Routledge Revivals

Foundations of Faith Volume 1

Originally published in 1924, this is the first of four volumes to discuss Christian Theology, under the guidance of the historic decisions of the Christian Church and the prevailing tendencies of Catholic thought in the early 20th Century. This volume deals with the fundamental groundwork of Thesim.

Foundations of Faith Volume 1
Theological

W.E. Orchard

First published in 1924 by George Allen & Unwin Ltd.

This edition first published in 2024 by Routledge
4 Park Square, Milton Park, Abingdon, Oxon, OX14 4RN

and by Routledge
605 Third Avenue, New York, NY 10158.

Routledge is an imprint of the Taylor & Francis Group, an informa business

© 1924 W.E. Orchard.

The right of W.E. Orchard to be identified as the author of this work has been asserted by him in accordance with sections 77 and 78 of the Copyright, Designs and Patents Act 1988.

All rights reserved. No part of this book may be reprinted or reproduced or utilised in any form or by any electronic, mechanical, or other means, now known or hereafter invented, including photocopying and recording, or in any information storage or retrieval system, without permission in writing from the publishers.

ISBN 13: 978-1-032-89951-0 (hbk)
ISBN 13: 978-1-003-54550-7 (ebk)
ISBN 13: 978-1-032-89959-6 (pbk)
Book DOI 10.4324/9781003545507

FOUNDATIONS OF FAITH

I
THEOLOGICAL

BY THE
REV. W. E. ORCHARD, D.D.

LONDON: GEORGE ALLEN & UNWIN LTD.
RUSKIN HOUSE, 40 MUSEUM STREET, W.C.1

First Published in 1924

(*All rights reserved.*)

Printed in Great Britain by
UNWIN BROTHERS, LIMITED, THE GRESHAM PRESS, LONDON AND WOKING

CONTENTS

	PAGE
THE EXISTENCE OF GOD	1
CAN MAN KNOW GOD?	17
THE NATURE OF GOD	33
CREATION	49
EVOLUTION AND THE FALL	65
HUMAN FREEDOM AND RESPONSIBILITY	81
PROVIDENCE AND GRACE	97
THE PROBLEM OF EVIL	113
PRAYER AND ITS DIFFICULTIES	129
MIRACLES	145
THE INSTINCT FOR RELIGION	161
COMPARATIVE RELIGION	177

CORRECTIONS

On page 144 (line 3) thanksgiving should be added to the elements of prayer.

On page 154, Newton's Law of Gravitation is only used as an illustration, and is therefore stated roughly; but in its exact form it should of course read:

Masses are drawn to one another in proportion to the product of their masses and in inverse proportion to the square of their distance.

I

THE EXISTENCE OF GOD

IS there a God? *Apparently* not. That is to say, God is not apparent to our senses. Then if God is not apparent to our senses, is He apparent to our observation, to our mere reflective perception? The scientific method never directly observes God; all its experiments only reveal the action of natural forces. Scientific analysis may reduce living matter to its inorganic elements; life itself eludes analysis, and no artificial synthesis can create life, but no one proposes to identify this unknown element or quality with God; it may be His creation, but so may inorganic matter be.

When we turn to the observation of history, are there any events which reveal the immediate and indisputable action of God? This is to raise the question of miracle, which at present we must leave aside. There have been many events in the past, and some even nearer at hand, which have been regarded as due solely to the immediate operation of God; but there will always be a difference of opinion on this matter, not only because it is questionable how far historical evidence is trustworthy, but because even if we had direct and immediate evidence, many would refer the event to natural but unknown causes; to them the absence of a known natural cause would not prove the real cause to be God.

Then is God apparent to reason? If we take the world as a whole, does it demand God as its only possible explanation? If we look at human history, does it clearly indicate the guidance of God? That is to say, is God the only explanation of existence which satisfies reason? We cannot expect that an affirmative answer will rise to more than the highest kind of probability; it will fall short of absolute demonstration; but only because there is no such thing possible in our present state of knowledge. The existence of God may be the strongest probability in life; from the nature of the case, we cannot expect it to be anything more. Lest the believer in God should feel dissatisfied with this position, or the unbeliever regard it as sufficient to warrant his remaining in unbelief, let both remind themselves that other things of only slightly less importance are in exactly the same case. For instance: the existence of the soul is something which cannot be absolutely proved. We are not referring to the immortality of the human soul, but only to the existence of something distinct from our bodies and even from our thoughts; that something referred to when we say "I." Most people are quite certain that when they say "I" they mean something more than a series of thoughts which is conveniently labelled "I." Thinking involves a conscious personal subject: it is not our thinking which we label "I," it is "I" who do the thinking. All this, however, is a matter of inference; and some thinkers—Hume for instance—have declared that they were never conscious of this "I," but only of certain sensations and thoughts; though even Hume could not state his position without referring to the person who was conscious of these things.

And when we come to the existence of the world, although there is almost no human being who is not perfectly certain that there is a world outside himself, it is exceedingly difficult to prove. We all assume the existence of outside things without further inquiry; it is only when we ask for proof that we find there is very little. The proof of the existence of God is therefore in no worse case than the existence of the soul, or the world. We are immediately conscious of the outside world; we *infer* the existence of our souls, because nothing else explains our activities and our experience; and we infer the existence of God, because nothing less explains our souls and the world taken together. It is this last statement which we have to examine, and we shall find it most convenient to examine first of all the hypothesis that it is not true.

Let us suppose that God does not exist. If there is no God, then the existence of the world must be self-explained. It is conceivable that the world, as we see it to-day, has evolved, that it has grown richer, more complex, and has produced higher forms of life merely from the powers inherent in its component elements. But to whatever simple form of existence we can conceive the whole might be traced back, it is inconceivable that by any process it could be traced back to nothing at all. Some philosophers and scientists are apparently able to conceive that the existence of the world might be deduced from the existence of matter and force only. It would take us too far afield to examine whether we have very definite ideas of what we mean by either; but can we regard them as needing no further explanation? It seems clear that there can be no motion without matter; we can, however, conceive matter without motion. Matter, then, seems to be the more original. Then motion came later. Where from? It cannot have come from nothing. There is no escape by assuming that motion is an inherent quality of matter, because if so, whenever matter may have started to move by its inherent quality, it ought obviously to have started before; otherwise, motion is being reduced eventually to non-motion, and that which originally did not move began to move of itself, which is absurd. Nor is there any escape in the suggestion that motion is the more original and is eternal, It is impossible to conceive motion without matter. Moreover, the movement of matter has changed its rate of motion; and to assume that movement has gone on in cycles, spending itself till it gets exhausted and everything dies down into inertia, and then beginning from this inertia to work up greater and more complicated movement, is simply to increase the absurdity of motion constantly able to begin without anything to start it. Even if matter were eternal, motion must come from some non-material source, and the only other source we can conceive of is that of mind. We know that our minds have the power of inducing motion; motion can therefore be most reasonably referred to mind. The hypothesis that matter is nothing but motion seems inconceivable; but if matter were nothing but motion, then everything would be only the more easily traceable to mind. It is this hypothesis of original and originating mind which is, however, resisted. Can we get on without it?

Let us pass over the difficulties which we have found in the idea that all existence can be sufficiently accounted for by matter and motion, which do not themselves need to be accounted for, and for a moment accept the idea that these are sufficient, and the world therefore started without mind, which has only evolved later. This means that evolution began without purpose, for purpose is an attribute of mind. For evolving mind to attempt to impose its purpose on the world is ultimately impossible, for however mind may alter the dispositions and directions of matter and motion, there will always be something in them that will finally resist that purpose, for on this hypothesis, they came into existence before and apart from mind. Now the mind of man has desires, and it tries to alter the world according to these desires. By studying the laws of matter and motion it can considerably alter the face of things and the character of life. And yet no alterations we can ever make will completely satisfy these desires. In fact, the more changes we make, the more the mind awakes to its own dissatisfaction. Therefore we are faced with this intolerable position, that matter and motion have given rise to something quite alien to them, without which matter and motion would have no meaning, and yet which they themselves can never satisfy. A further fact gradually presses itself upon us: that our mind has no companion. It cannot find satisfaction in the world of things; but, strangely enough, it cannot find satisfaction in other minds, whether this be sought in the affection of another single mind, or in the vast output of the human mind stored in literature. For these other minds only communicate their unsatisfied desires, and add their burden to ours; while the study of literature or art only intensifies our desires and makes us more discontented with things. Nor does the future hold any better hope for humanity; not only is there the fact that individuals die with their desires unsatisfied, but the whole human race will either eventually die out or will grow increasingly miserable. We are bound, therefore, to reject the hypothesis of a world which started without purpose, and in which mind gradually emerged, because it involves not only the complete frustration of human desire, but the worthlessness of mind itself. We are compelled to question whether the mind which emerges from, and finds itself in, such an alien world, can possibly understand the world. This means we are compelled to doubt the capacity of our reason, and in consequence the theory that mind comes from matter and motion; we have seen it is unreasonable in itself, and it ends by discrediting the reason on which it is based. Even those who cannot see how this position stands self-condemned, can see the condition in which it leaves us. The position entailed by denying the existence of God so appals the mind that men propose at least some kind of substitute. Now these substitutes can be shown to be not only inadequate, but to involve the same hopeless position more or less skilfully concealed.

The immortality of the race has been proposed as a substitute for the immortality of the soul; but science holds out little hope of the immortality of the race on this earth, and even if it were guaranteed, there is no assurance that the human race would not destroy itself. The idea is therefore being advanced that man's spirit is immortal, but that there is no higher being: immortality is being proposed as a substitute for God. Now this simply takes into another life all the problems of the present life, and intensifies them; because

THE EXISTENCE OF GOD

although we may imagine that it is earthly conditions and our present fleshly habitat which constitute the misery of the soul, it is really the soul itself that is miserable, because it can find no companion. Immortality without God would only be another name for hell. The attempt is sometimes made to relieve the situation by the idea of an inevitable progress for every soul. But there is not the slightest guarantee of this in anything we know from human history or our individual experience; progress can only come by our realizing some higher principle of life, and discovering some higher power than we ourselves possess. The necessity for some higher being than man, who can be man's companion, helper and goal, is therefore felt by many; and so they suggest approximations to the idea of God, which also prove inadequate; because they are still nothing but atheism politely concealed under the notion of something borrowed from the idea of God. For instance, the existence of an impersonal purpose is proposed as sufficient. We often talk about the purpose of nature; but nothing can have a purpose but a mind, and if nature has a purpose, it is because there is a mind behind it. Sometimes this principle is denominated by some abstraction like Goodness or Love; but goodness and love are attributes of mind and cannot exist without. Goodness and love exist in humanity, and humanity could increase them; but the emergence of these qualities is more explicable and their increase more likely if there is some source of goodness and love above humanity constantly acting upon it. If there is, this superior goodness and love must be an attribute of some superior mind.

The same objection holds good against the

proposal of Reason as a sufficient principle for the guidance of man. Whenever men appeal to Reason, they appeal not only to something in the mind of man, but to something to which the mind ought to submit itself and, therefore, to something above the mind. Reason is an ideal which man strives after; and this involves that Reason is something which exists above and beyond man's mind; if it does, it must be an attribute of a higher mind. Moreover, we have shown that without this higher Reason being the origin of things, reason emerging later in an irrational scheme would have no ground for being regarded as trustworthy.

Can anything be said for the proposed substitute, which is quite a modern one, that although God does not now exist, He will come into existence in the future through the action of the human consciousness; that just as the material world has produced mind, so mind will at length produce God? This is an even worse example of the absurd notion that nothing can produce something. The God who is thus brought into existence will be an alien, and there is no hope that He will ever be able to do anything to impress His purpose on the world or upon humanity. If matter has created man, man is only material, and then the mind which creates God makes God Himself only material. Not only does this conception utterly deny what is implied by the word "God," but such a God can be of no help to us, even when He comes into existence. The theory that God does not exist therefore offers no explanation of existence, undermines the very reason which seeks to establish this theory, and contradicts our highest hopes and desires.

In logic, when of two contradictories one is

proved to be impossible, the other is taken to be true. We have shown that the negative answer to the question, Is there a God? is improbable and incredible. Is this sufficient to establish the alternative that God exists? This would be so if we had sufficiently definite ideas of what is meant by God. But there are obviously *three* possible answers to the problem of existence: (1) Existence is due to natural causes. This we have seen to be improbable. (2) Existence is due to some being or power which may be inferred from the nature of existence. This would lead us to infer a being of immense mind and vast power; but it might tell us nothing more than that. (3) Existence is due to the God set forth by the Christian religion. Our choice must be between (2) and (3). If the nature of the Being to whom existence is to be traced is to be inferred from existence, this will be an inductive argument, and in addition to the comparative uncertainty of the inductive method, it will give us just so much as and no more than existence demands; whereas it is conceivable that God may be much greater than visible existence and the natural order demand. The deductive method is more certain and convincing, but it entails that we must assume the existence of God to begin with. Moreover, the Christian religion does not allow that created existence can be deduced from the mere existence of God; for it holds that creation is the free act of His will, and neither a necessary activity of His Being nor an emanation of His essence. Yet the two methods are not exclusive or antagonistic. Arguing from existence alone, enough may be established concerning God to confirm the revelation of the Christian religion, and to make it a natural and credible completion of what reason can establish by itself. This is all that is claimed: namely, that the existence of the world requires us to believe in the existence of a Being of vast mind and power, whom man is bound by the use of his reason to acknowledge, to seek to know Him and to enter into relationship with Him, and so to welcome the revelation which God has made of Himself; which, although reason could not have reached, reason does prepare us to expect, and when received finds to be rational.

With these conditions in mind, we now seek to establish the existence of God by positive argument; and the first argument for the existence of God is based upon the fact of external motion.

We have seen that even the idea of the simplest movement of matter seems to require a source outside matter itself, and that source non-material. But that would only take us to the idea of force or energy; and some seem able to rest content in that, as if it were a self-explanatory thing; whereas the only force we know immediately is due to our minds. We are, moreover, not arguing from physical force, as such, to the existence of God, but from the actual kind of motion to which this force gives rise: for the motion of the universe develops into what we call evolution. Evolution, like motion, of which it is only a complicated form, is often taken to be self-explanatory, whereas it is the thing to be explained. That things in this world move to a higher stage of development by small steps spread over vast time is no explanation. Not only is the mere fact of change, however small, in need of explanation, but the fact that the change is in an upward direction is still more so. All the motion with which we are acquainted gradually grows less and less. We are also accustomed to the possibility of a higher form of life deteriorating into a lower; that is what is perpetually happening in the world of nature when left untended by man. Therefore, if the present existing world, with man as its present highest production, has simply developed from some lower form and state, that development must need more explanation than the mere existence of motion. It is no longer held by scientific evolutionists that the upward motion of existence is due merely to natural selection: there is about all organic life a restlessness that is continuously seeking change, which is the very characteristic of life. Now is this inner restlessness quite arbitrary, while there is something else acting from without which selects from the changes produced under this impulse those which make for advance? These two forces of inner tendency and external selection cannot account for evolution. The external force which makes for selection must act according to a purpose; for the tiny changes made by the creature's restlessness are not recognisably favourable to its existence until they reach a much higher stage of development. In short, behind the creature's restlessness, and behind the action of its environment upon it, which draws out its impulse and selects those changes which are favourable, there is a purpose; and purpose involves a conscious mind. That mind is neither in the creature nor in the external processes, but while working through them both, must be above them both.

Therefore the fact of evolution which was once thought to dispense with God really demands God all the more, and involves Him not merely at the beginning, but as constantly working through the process; and it demands a God at least adequate to this process.

THE EXISTENCE OF GOD

The second argument is built upon the nature and movement of the soul.

We have seen that the personal pronoun "I" stands for something distinct from, though functioning in and through, the body; even distinct from the sensations derived from the world without; for it is the subject of them, and is even distinct from its own thoughts, which are only its activity and expression. This personal ego is an immaterial as well as an invisible reality. That it is of a different nature from the body may be seen from the fact that its activities are incapable of being stated in material terms. Material things can be measured and weighed: the activities of the soul cannot. We often speak of our thoughts being deep, or long, or depressed; but these are only metaphors; for the moment we ask How long? How deep? we know we are asking foolish questions. Even the physical sensations which are registered by the mind are not registered in a merely physical way. We can measure cold by an instrument; we can only measure colour by the mind; for although the sensation of blue is caused by waves of light which can be measured, there is an entire difference between waves of light and the sensation we call blue. And when we come to our thoughts, all talk of measurement is now out of the question. It is possible to open a man's head and look at his brain, and it is conceivable that by some delicate instrument we might detect some movement in the particles of his brain; we certainly could detect the increase of heat which showed that his brain was at work, but we should not be able to see what he was thinking about. On the other hand, a man can be conscious of his thoughts, of the order in which thoughts come, the purpose he has in following a certain line of thought or the conclusions which he believes to be sound, and yet he will be quite unconscious of that movement of his brain which the delicate instrument might be able to detect. All this shows the soul is an immaterial reality. In addition, there are certain movements of the soul which we call aspiration; this is its most characteristic motion. As the soul becomes aware of itself, it desires to be greater than itself. It is constantly aware of an ideal from which it can all too easily and painfully distinguish its actuality. That ideal registers itself even in the most careless soul as an intimation that it ought to be better; or, at the lowest, as a vague dissatisfaction with itself. But when the soul sets out to investigate by inquiry what this ideal demands of it, it discovers that the demand is practically endless; if the soul endeavours to lift itself up in order to correspond with its ideal, then the ideal only more rapidly reveals still higher demands. These demands at length resolve themselves into nothing short of perfection, and since the idea of perfection itself continually advances under response to these demands, and the goodness which the soul desires reveals itself to be boundless, it discovers that the ideal is infinite. Now it is as difficult to see how the soul itself could have created this ideal as it is to explain how matter could come from nothing and motion originate from the inert. The only possible explanation of the pressure of this ideal, as it is revealed by examination, is that it is due to the activity of an ideal being.

This twofold argument from the movement in the world outside and the movement in our own souls seems to establish the existence of God as the only possible explanation of them both. From the soul itself, its nature and activity, we can conceive how a higher form of immaterial being could act invisibly upon the world after the analogy of the soul's action upon the body. God is therefore not only shown to exist, but something of His nature and activity can be conceived.

Now, as a matter of fact, belief in the existence of a God is very widespread; it is found not only amongst civilized, but among savage peoples, and as far back as we can penetrate into history. It can therefore be claimed to be practically universal; wherever it has been at first thought to be non-existent, closer research has discovered its existence; wherever any attempt has been made to ignore or challenge this belief, it has only called forth a stronger reaction on the other side. The very existence of the idea of God is a strong presupposition of something real corresponding to it. We cannot argue directly from the idea of God to His existence, as if the idea itself proved His existence; but it is exceedingly difficult to discover any other cause for the emergence of the idea, save that it is true; and all the more since God is invisible. Various attempts have been made to derive the idea of God from ancestor worship, belief in ghosts, or a fallacious animistic argument; but since the respective exponents of each of these rival theories have successfully demolished the others, these attempts may be regarded as entirely unsuccessful. Moreover, it is obvious that the acutest form of reasoning by which we to-day endeavour to establish the existence of God is only the sharpening of an unconscious process by which man has come to believe in God through his observation of the world without and the feelings which arise within his own soul. The argument from the idea of God to His existence cannot, taken alone, be regarded as a proof, yet with the universality of the idea borne in mind, the impossibility of tracing it to any other source, together with the fact that the application of reason has only purified and strengthened the idea, it does bring a confirmation to the two other arguments, and makes the existence of God as strong a cumulative possibility as is possible in the nature of things, or is needed for reasonable belief. These arguments, taken in conjunction with the appalling prospect which follows from the idea being untrue, considering the damaging verdict which must lie against all human thought if this idea is dismissed as a delusion, and weighing the impossibility of finding a basis for reason itself unless God is made the starting-point involved in all thought, constitute a probability so impressive, that not to believe in God wears an appearance of being due to resistance to the conclusions of reason for other than rational motives.

It may be admitted that there is an absence of such absolutely compelling demonstration as to leave the mind with no sort of choice; but, as we have seen, it is doubtful whether even the existence of ourselves or of things outside is in any better condition, or whether any such demonstration actually exists. If we assume things to exist, we must assume God; if we assume the possibility of rational thought, we must assume God; and these assumptions we cannot refuse, unless we are willing to land ourselves in absurdity, For in the one case we are bound to order our lives as if the outside world did exist; and we are bound to assume the rationality of human thought; since to say that everything is irrational implies some rational standard, and, like the statement that there is no such thing as truth, is refuted simply by stating it.

These arguments may still leave us without any consciousness of God, without any "feeling" that He is either real or near; but that is largely due to the fact that so few of us are accustomed to use our reason to establish anything. For the great majority the kind of argument which we have been following is one that is rarely used. But not only does the argument establish belief in God as reasonable, but it serves to give us faith in reason, and to strengthen our reasoning powers. It is not surprising, therefore, that in our own generation believers in God are almost the last rationalists. There is no longer any acceptable rationalistic objection to the existence of God; objection to-day comes rather from the thoughtless, or from those who, by their erratic methods of thought, or by actual confession, reveal themselves to be irrationalists. But when we have allowed these conclusions to carry the weight that they ought, when we have thought about them long and deeply, and if we go on to seek confirmation of our rational conclusions by shaping our lives in accordance with them, and by striving to get into conscious personal relationship with God, we shall find the idea of God growing clearer, our conviction stronger. Then, either by some sudden light within the mind, or by some gradual change of feeling, the intellectual conclusions may prepare the way for the conviction which is called faith: an absclute, unshakable assurance, in which the whole of one's nature joins and is thereby united, that GOD IS.

II

CAN MAN KNOW GOD?

ATHEISM is said to be getting rarer nowadays. It was probably never very widespread, and its public profession has always been unpopular. And the reason for this is obvious: no effort can make atheism other than a cheerless creed. Quite apart from the craving for God, which is so instinctive with man that, as Voltaire said, if there were not a God, we should have to invent one, the non-existence of God is gradually seen to involve the absence of any basis for human reason or human hopes. The evolution of mind from a mindless world gives no ground for assuming that human reason is capable of coming to any conclusions about the world. If the thoughts in the mind of man are simply the last term of a process which began without mind, and are rigorously determined by that process, the results of even the most exhaustive and persevering thought have no claim to be regarded as rational; they are simply the impressions made upon the most sensitive matter by the rest of matter; all thought has precisely the same value, for everything is then equally true, or rather, since this is impossible where there is such variety and contradiction, there is no standard of truth and the very word is without meaning. Whatever atheism is, it is a theory, and if it is true, there is no room for theories.

Moreover, to profess atheism carries with it the implication that one has examined the whole universe and has surveyed all the realms of knowledge; for this is necessary before one can commit oneself to the belief that there is no God. The public profession of atheism is, therefore, discovered to demand something more than courage; it needs arrogance and sheer bravado. But its secret admission is not only as difficult; it is also dangerous. It is so contrary to man's instinctive tendency that its natural effect is to waken internal resistance; the deliberate adoption of such an extreme denial carries such appalling conclusions that one is the more likely to be frightened into the opposite belief. For atheism involves that there is no being superior to man, which, instead of exalting man, must at last deprive him of all hope.

Our generation is no longer able to take refuge in the idea of inevitable human progress. Even if the mind of man has developed from mindless material, this unguided mind can make a terrible use of its knowledge and power. Education can end in the increase of egoism, with consequent strife without and misery within, and the lessening likelihood of men ever coming to agree about anything. Scientific knowledge and invention can be used to destroy life as easily as aid and rescue it; and the multiplication of riches, the mass production of necessities, and the cheapening of luxuries can end in the increase of degrading poverty, enslaving toil, and the prospect of starvation as the inevitable result of industrial development. Even the desires for social reform, the most hopeful sign of our times, seem only to generate further disagreement, strife and hate, and promise to end either in tyranny or anarchy. If man is the supreme being, one cannot even say, as one is inclined to : God help him !

Therefore atheism, if it any longer exists, is unprofessed and unadmitted; but we can have no assurance that it is not the working creed and the practical belief of many; indirectly there is plenty of evidence that modern civilization is run on a basis of practical atheism. It were better that more were professed and violent atheists; the reaction would come all the sooner.

But another reason why atheism is so rarely professed is that its place has been largely taken by agnosticism; though the fact that a man calls himself an agnostic is no evidence that he knows what he means by it. For the truth is that the term is ambiguous. A man can declare he is an agnostic, meaning simply that he does not know whether there is a God or not. He neither affirms nor denies; he says only, " I do not know." Now this may be true as a statement of his immediate mental condition, but he can hardly proclaim this condition as his creed. Therefore the person who calls himself an agnostic generally means more than this : he generally means that he regards the subject as one on which knowledge is impossible. This is theoretical agnosticism : the theory that God cannot be known by man.

These two positions demand separate examination. The simpler agnostic position is, as we have seen, only a personal confession ; but there is always a tendency for it to become the universal statement, " Man does not know God," and then for this ignorance to be defended by the dogmatic assertion that man *cannot* know God. The simpler agnosticism was professed by Huxley; the more philosophical system by Spencer. But even in so cautious a thinker as Huxley we can see the one position passing over into the other. Speaking of his fellow-members of the Metaphysical Society, Huxley says: "They were quite certain that they had attained a certain 'gnosis,' had more or less successfully solved the problem of existence; while I was quite sure that I had not, and had a pretty strong conviction that the problem was insoluble." Two things have to be noticed about this now famous statement. Firstly, it refers generally to the solution of the problem of existence, and not specifically to the existence of God. But, of course, the existence of God is such a factor in any possible solution that we may take the wider reference to include the narrower, as it did for Huxley. Secondly, the personal confession passes over into the conviction that the problem is insoluble. Many convinced and devout believers would admit with Huxley that existence contains many unsolved problems, but they would regard the assertion that any problem was insoluble as not only too confident a despair, but as involving an unscientific statement and an unphilosophical position. They would be rather inclined to say that it is precisely when the existence of God is not admitted that existence becomes an insoluble problem; for since all visible existence is contingent, it can only be explained by that which is self-existent, and which, therefore, needs no further explanation.

That there must be such a self-existent Being is the starting-point of Herbert Spencer's type of agnosticism. It needs to be remembered that this, the only systematic exposition of agnosticism, makes the existence of God its very starting-point and the indisputable basis of all thought. We ought to notice that Spencer prefers to call God the Absolute, and this is an ambiguous term, which may give rise to some confusion. The Absolute might be taken to mean that which exists out of relation to anything else; when, of course, we could know nothing whatever about it. It is sometimes taken to mean the totality of things in distinction from its parts; when it would be readily admitted by anyone that the totality must exist, but that to know the totality of things is impossible for any human being. We must, of course, dissociate the term from the association which the word has come to convey through its use in an "absolute" monarchy; for this has obviously motived some objections to the idea of the Absolute. But Spencer means by the Absolute that which is not relative, namely, the Self-existing. Therefore, for our present purpose we may take his discussion concerning the Absolute to bear upon our question of whether man can know God.

Now Spencer argues that the existence of the Absolute is a necessity for all thought. All our sense of anything being relative is due to our still deeper sense of something being absolute. This is an important conclusion, and is in contradiction to the widespread idea that our notion of the infinite, for instance, is simply a negation of the finite, which is all that we can have any positive notion of. Spencer holds that it is the infinite which is the positive idea, of which the finite is merely the negation. It needs profound reflection to see the truth of this, and the demonstration of it is beyond our concern; but it needs to be remembered that this is the basis of Spencer's agnosticism: " though the Absolute cannot in any manner or degree be known, in the strict sense of knowing, yet we find that its positive existence is a necessary datum of consciousness, that as long as consciousness continues, we cannot for an instant rid it of its datum: and that thus the belief which the datum constitutes has a higher warrant than any other whatever." This is a most valuable admission: and it is to be wondered how many agnostics agree with it, or even know of its existence.

Yet it is on this irrefutable conclusion that the Absolute exists that Spencer declares it is unknowable: "the Absolute cannot in any manner or degree be known." It involves an extraordinary position to affirm that something exists about which nothing further can be known. To know that anything exists we must know what kind of a thing it is; that is we must know something about it. Spencer knows that this existing somewhat is the Absolute, that is that it is self-existing. But that is to know a great deal about it: in fact, what we most need to know. Elsewhere Spencer admits that this inscrutable power (which is still another item of knowledge: the Absolute is a power) is manifested to us through all phenomena. The Absolute, therefore, has its manifestations; and surely this gives us ample material for knowing a great deal about God.

At this point we may register an agreement between agnosticism and Christianity. It may be as unknown to some agnostics that Christian theology admits that God cannot be known as He is in Himself, but only so far as He has manifested Himself, as it may be that Spencer has admitted that the Unknowable has its manifestations. But there is an even further admission:

CAN MAN KNOW GOD?

Spencer declares that this inscrutable power is the same as that which wells up within our own consciousness. Now our own consciousness is that of which we have the most immediate and certain knowledge; here, then, is still more material for our knowledge of God.

Probably this Spencerian agnosticism is too positive in its basis, and makes too many admissions as to the knowability of the Absolute to satisfy many modern agnostics. But before we leave this system to discuss whether any other agnostic position is more tenable, we might inquire in what sense, then, Spencer thinks God is unknowable. He has given the hint in the sentence quoted above. He says the Absolute cannot be known "in the strict sense of knowing." What is this strict sense of knowing, with which any possible knowledge of God is so unfavourably contrasted? It cannot be scientific knowledge, for Spencer looks forward to a time when "Science becomes convinced that its explanations are proximate and relative, while religion becomes convinced that the mystery it contemplates is ultimate and absolute." And philosophical knowledge, that is, the certainty of intellectual conclusions, would hardly satisfy the religious mind and the craving for a manifestation of God. It looks, therefore, as if some ideal and non-existent knowledge was being set up, and then any knowledge which religion might attain dismissed as worthless because it was not like that. But here another agreement between agnosticism and religious thought may be registered. The Bible asks: "Canst thou find out the Almighty to perfection?" and answers: "How unsearchable are His judgments, and His ways past tracing out!" and yet declares that "that which may be known of God is manifest," while it sanctions the paradoxical desire to "know the love ... which passeth knowledge," and "the peace ... which passeth all understanding."

The truth is we can know some things intuitively which we, nevertheless, cannot define, such as life, love, truth; indeed, all the greatest things are thus known. We can know a thing as a whole which we do not know in part, and which we therefore could not describe. A man would not be denied knowledge of his wife because he could not draw her face, or describe her sufficiently to enable anyone else to identify her. Knowledge may be quite sufficient for common life and certain action, which is at the same time intellectually inadequate and confused. It would be difficult to say where blue ended and green began in the spectrum, and one might be doubtful whether any given colour was to be described as blue or green; but that would hardly be a sufficient indication that a person did not know the difference between blue and green. There are many things we know which we do not understand. We can often find our way to a place to which we should hardly know how to direct anyone else; there are many things we know how to do, but could not tell how we do them. These well-known facts serve to show that we may have a knowledge of God which is neither scientific nor theologically accurate, which may nevertheless be sufficient to enable us to worship, to love and to serve Him.

On the one hand, then, the philosophy of the Unknowable admits that the Absolute exists; that it is a power; that it is manifested through phenomena; that it is the same as that which wells up in our consciousness. On the other hand, religion admits that God is only knowable in so far as He has revealed Himself, that our knowledge is necessarily imperfect, yet not thereby necessarily erroneous; that we may know God more intimately than our arguments, our definitions, our descriptions might be taken to indicate.

The position, therefore, that God is unknowable is untenable: it is pure dogmatism; it is due to confusion; and the attempt to maintain it only ends in such qualifications and admissions as to make it self-refuting.

We have therefore reached the position in which it is clear that we cannot say man cannot know God. That leaves open the only alternative; man can know God. If this is so, then it is a man's duty to seek God, if haply he may find Him, though he is not far from any one of us. It therefore does not look even possible for any retreat to be made to the simpler position where anyone can say, "whatever position others may be in, I do not know God." Ignorance may be our condition, and indeed the awareness of our ignorance may be the very beginning of knowledge, a sign of humility, and a spur to the pursuit of knowledge. But no man could remain content with this ignorance if knowledge were open to him; least of all glory in it and make it his only religious confession. It is even questionable whether a man can confidently say, "I do not know God," even as the confession of a temporary condition; for if the philosophical defence of agnosticism is not open to him, namely the proof that God is unknowable, even the assertion that he personally does not know God begins to look uncertain.

Before a man can truthfully say, "I do not know God," he must have searched his own mind and made certain that there is no trace of any knowledge of God contained in it. There may be something we know, but have forgotten. So long as it remains forgotten it is useless knowledge, but it may be brought to mind again. There may be something we know, but do not know that we know. That is unrealized but not inaccessible knowledge; for it may be found to be involved in what we really do know. Now when a man says he does not know God, does it mean that he does not know what the idea means; that he has no notion of God in his mind; that he does not know whether the notion has any reality corresponding to it; or merely, that, while he has such an idea, and believes there is something corresponding to it, he does not know God personally, that is in any certain, effective and intimate way?

No one can say he has no idea of God in his mind. Mankind has always had some idea of God; and everyone has some conception of a being superior to man as at least possible. This admission is not to be turned by demanding to know first what someone else's idea of God is, and then saying it is not ours; asking for an agreed complete definition of God before any decision as to His existence can be made. The idea of something superior to man himself is an inalienable element in human consciousness. It is the cause of our own sense of imperfection and shortcoming, as it is also the cause of our continual criticism of our fellows. We are constantly complaining that men are so wicked, untruthful, mean, stupid; fresh indications of this are always taking us by surprise and causing us astonishment and pain. It might, indeed, be said that it is this something better than man that we best know and understand, and that it is man that is the mystery. Our self-knowledge, in short, involves the knowledge of something above ourselves. Now if we only inquire as to what sort of a being would content us, we should find that it would have to be morally perfect. The idea of moral perfection is the most fundamental and fruitful idea in our minds, yet we refuse to examine it, we try to run away from it and forget it, because it raises such pressing questions and contains in its contrast with what we are such possibility of pain. It is beyond all possibility that we have ourselves invented this idea; it is too active and too painful to be our own manufacture. It is more than an idea; it is an energy of which our minds are aware; it is the pressure upon us of active, and therefore actually existing moral perfection. Our present purpose is not moral exhortation; but if this fact could only be given full weight to and seriously examined, it would reveal to anyone who attempted it how intimately and wonderfully he knew God. The knowledge of God is therefore involved in man's moral consciousness; his knowledge of himself reveals his knowledge of God. It is only the moral distress which this knowledge occasions which leads to its being ignored and repressed.

But not only does man know God in knowing himself, he knows God better than he knows himself, for he only knows himself by knowing God. This can be the only explanation of our being such a moral mystery to ourselves. We are this because we are more intimately aware of that moral perfection which God is; for, of course, there can be no such thing as abstract moral perfection; moral perfection is only predicable of conscious being.

Once this is seen, it is impossible to take refuge in the notion that we could have the idea of God in our mind without there being any reality attaching to it. It is this idea which bears every mark of reality, and which nothing else can explain.

Our scientific knowledge reveals to us how dependent everything is and how relative is all our knowledge. But our minds refuse to consider the idea that everything is really dependent upon everything else; we immediately ask, then what is everything dependent upon? Nor can we seriously entertain the notion that everything is dependent upon something higher and prior in an infinite and regressive series. The idea of a Self-Existent Being, Himself infinite, is the real answer to that puzzle. These two ideas of the morally perfect and the self-existent Being are seen to be one, because our moral ideas are obviously imperfect and dependent upon the morally self-existent, that is, the morally perfect; and since they cannot be dependent upon a mere moral abstraction or impersonal ideal, the morally perfect must be the self-existent Being, and the self-existent Being must be morally perfect.

Nor is this conclusion to be turned by the declaration that all our knowledge must be relative, and, therefore, can never include the knowledge of God. The question arises from the very statement that all our knowledge is relative: relative to what? The very sense of its relativity betrays that it is so because it has knowledge of the Absolute. If this knowledge is contrasted with scientific or sensible knowledge, there is no longer any possibility of regarding the latter as the superior knowledge. It is the knowledge of God which makes all other knowledge possible. Not only do we know God

CAN MAN KNOW GOD?

better than anything else, it is God alone that we truly know. And we have seen that so far from being able to know that God exists and yet know nothing about Him, we really know God, and, therefore, know that He exists.

The argument so far put forward is really a refutation of agnosticism by showing that, as a thought-out philosophy, it is untenable; that what it contains of truth, religion in general, and Christianity in particular, acknowledges and embodies; and that it contains admissions which compel us to go beyond its own circumscribed limits. But this may still fall short of converting a negative into a positive conviction. The earnest thinker may be convinced that a negative or even a neutral position is impossible. But that does not of itself bring a knowledge of God which can be described as certain, intimate, personal. It needs to be noted, however, that it is something gained to have cleared away objections. That will enable and encourage an advance to be attempted. But that advance will be made, and be likely to meet with success, only if there is some impelling need; if one feels some real desire for a clearer knowledge of God. Nothing is more fruitless than the endeavour to impart knowledge to those who do not want it: it often only puts up a resistance to its reception, and leads to its repression. This question should be decided before any further advance is seriously attempted. Truth cannot be sought without some sense of the need of truth, nor be found without strong desire for it. But suppose that some need for a further assurance of God's existence, and closer acquaintance with Him is felt, we can then set out upon our search with energy and confidence.

The fact that some knowledge of God is involved

in all knowledge needs to be thought about deeply and its significance carefully estimated. We can miss some of the most important things in life, we can overlook some of the most fundamental facts in our minds, simply through lack of attention. It is perfectly logical to argue that if God is going to be the goal of our search, He must be also in some degree the start. We shall never get out of thought what is not already involved in it. We cannot start from nowhere, if we hope to get anywhere. Even the most philosophical form of agnosticism has admitted that the Absolute is the datum of consciousness, that God is the beginning of all thought. If this is reflected on it will gradually change the whole direction of our minds. It is this starting-point which has been ignored, because it is inescapable and fundamental, and because it shows that we begin our search at all only because God has already in some measure revealed Himself to us; which is what we do not want to admit because of what it involves. But by turning in upon ourselves we discover God actually in our minds, not simply far away at the end of some distant process. The more this is considered the surer and nearer God is seen to be. There is, however, a danger in stopping at this discovery, momentous as it is. We may be inclined to think of God as only inside us and to look for Him elsewhere to regard as useless and unnecessary; and thereby incur the danger of making our own minds the sufficient measure of God, and, perhaps, then proceeding to the terrible mistake of identifying ourselves with God. To correct and avoid this, we must look for God beyond ourselves.

Anyone touched with the spirit of genuine agnosticism will be the less likely to fall into this pure subjectivism because there will always remain the haunting fear that while our own ideas and the working of our minds shuts us up to God, God is nothing more than our idea, and simply the inevitable product of our mental machinery, which need not itself be trustworthy. Yet entirely to distrust our mind is quite impossible; for we are compelled to use it to think at all; and to conclude that our mind was untrustworthy would entail that we must trust its verdict; which lands us in an absurd contradiction. But we do long for confirmation of the reality of our ideas. We can find this confirmation partly in the world without us: its vastness, order and beauty do confirm our idea of God as its only sufficient cause. We find some confirmation in the idea of God which others possess. The great seers, prophets and teachers of religion give to us a considerable assurance. But does not this only prove that all human minds work alike? Not entirely. The very fact of divergence and power, of variety and even contradiction, show us that there is freedom of choice, and room for the factors of special revelation, moral response and consistent character. If we select the idea of God which has made for comprehensiveness, for centrality, and for a clue to the other ideas; if we ask where this has developed along the most fruitful and effective line; where it has been accompanied by the most consistent and creative character; we find that it lies along the line that leads up to and develops from Christianity. And Christianity sets forth a unique revelation: that of the Incarnation. An Incarnation is demanded on agnostic principles if agnosticism is ever to be transcended: God must come to us, make Himself known by a revelation all can trust.

CAN MAN KNOW GOD?

We are in need of confirmation of the belief, not that the human mind can climb to God, but that God can reveal Himself in and through a human mind; for that is the doubt which gives rise to agnosticism. This can only be removed if we can see in history a person who not only reveals God, but is Himself a revelation of God. If the character, the claims and the career of Christ are considered, He will be found to be the most wonderful confirmation of the idea of God, as that can be expressed in human terms; as it must be if we are ever to be sure of God.

Moreover, Christianity does not present us with a God of whom there is nothing more to be revealed. The idea of God in Christianity is of One who still transcends our comprehension and always will. It does not profess to contain no mysteries: it has many; nor to leave no problems; some it even increases. But it gives us enough to trust for what remains unrevealed and unresolved. God, as He is in Himself, no Christian pretends to know: but only God as revealed. But what is revealed in Christ is so essential and personal, that although it may be extended to infinity, and must be, it will never be contradicted. It is in that sense sufficient and final. It reveals God so that there is nothing more that need be misunderstood, even if there remains much not yet understood. If from this revelation we turn again to science and philosophy, to history and experience, we find these have now a greater meaning, and they in turn confirm what we now know. We may still know only in part, and still through a glass darkly; but we have enough for faith, for hope and for love.

III

THE NATURE OF GOD

IT has been declared that it is not the existence of God that is in dispute, but His nature, of which there is no agreed definition; it is not *whether* God is, but *what* He is. First define God, and then it can be decided whether it is a consistent idea, and whether there is any reality corresponding to it. But if the definition demanded is to be logical and complete, this is impossible, for God cannot be so defined. God cannot be defined by comparative classification, because there is no higher class, and God is the only one in that class. God can only be defined as unlike any other class, and, therefore, negatively. We can declare what the idea of God positively contains, but this will never be exhaustive, because we can only refer to Him those characteristics which He shares with others, but in a perfect degree; and what perfection is we cannot define. What God has which no one else has, as well as that which others have and He has not, must both be negative by definition. But although our definitions of God must be necessarily negative, inadequate and unimaginable, this does not mean that the reality to which we can rise only by negation is not itself positive. Moreover, theology does not shrink from the conclusion that God must transcend all our ideas of Him; it is the fact that He does that

THE NATURE OF GOD

constitutes Him God. All our definite ideas come to an end, but we never dream of claiming that our ideas exhaust reality; the very fact that they come to an end reveals to us that there is something still beyond them. Human thought is always a witness to something beyond itself, and if that something beyond itself is denied, then all human thought is reduced to a futility and an illusion. Neither do these necessary limitations to human thought make it impossible to know anything about the nature of God. We can know that God is all that He shares with other beings, all that is revealed through His works; and from the constitution of our own thought we can infer that He is much besides that which must surpass all manifestations as well as the highest conception that human thought can frame.

But if we are not hindered by rising above our own human thoughts by this negative method, neither need we start by assuming the existence of that perfection and infinity which seem actually to be involved in our consciousness, when all we see and feel and know falls so short of it. We can take a much simpler course and start from lower ground. If it can be admitted that man is not necessarily the highest type of being that might exist, then, however many ranks of being there may be above him, by God we mean simply the highest type or the Supreme Being, the Being than whom there is none higher. But there are persons who hold that man is the highest form of existing being. We are not now concerned with the refutation of that position, and so must content ourselves with pointing out that it is self-refuting, since man is a dependent being, and if he does not depend upon something higher than himself, he depends upon something lower; for instance, the merely physical universe; which involves us in the contradiction that the highest type of being depends on a type of being lower than itself. On the contrary, human consciousness bears continuous and inescapable witness to the existence of something higher than itself. The examination of our own conscious thought reveals that the infinite and the absolute is the standard by which we measure all else. If there is no reality corresponding to this, all human thought is a delusion, and we cannot rest in that conclusion, because to declare that everything is a delusion still involves that we have the conception of something which is not a delusion, but a reality. Then we have landed ourselves in another contradiction, for we can only declare that all is a delusion by comparison with the idea that something is not; whence all cannot be a delusion.

For the majority of us, however, it is not in these philosophical ideas, which all cannot even follow, but in the witness of our moral consciousness, that we are most aware of something higher than ourselves. We judge ourselves to be morally imperfect, and that must be because we have some idea of a moral nature superior to our own. This we cannot have derived from comparison with any other human being, since we have never known anyone in whom we could not recognize defects or suggest some possible improvement. Nor does it come from humanity as a whole, conceived as more perfect than any given individual, for it is mankind in the mass that we recognize to be constitutionally imperfect and lamentably lacking in rationality and goodness. There is no escape from this testimony of our moral consciousness by dismissing that the conception with which we contrast what we actually are as only an ideal. If this something higher than ourselves is only our own ideal, which we ourselves have created, then we are committed to the unnatural conclusion that the lesser can produce the greater, and only expose ourselves to the inquiry: Why is it that we can create a higher ideal, so much more easily than we can create a higher character? What can be rightly concluded from the declaration that the higher something which we can conceive is an ideal is that this higher something is not merely higher, but involves perfection and infinity.

There is no escape from the conclusion that the human mind is always conscious of something higher than itself, which is the very background of all its thought, that it continually conceives this higher as not only higher than itself, but higher than its highest possible thought; and so far from this being the creation of human thought, it discovers it to be above anything it can conceive. We thus find our thought rise to the idea of an infinitely transcending reality of whose existence we cannot really doubt, since to doubt this would be to doubt our own minds entirely, which is never possible. But for many people all such methods of introverted thought are very difficult, and the result appears to them vague, unsatisfactory and ineffective. We have, therefore, to see if we can learn something more of the nature of this reality by positive analogy.

The first material from which we can derive indisputable knowledge of the nature of God is contained in the fact of His invisibility. It is this fact which is the commonest stumbling-block to many minds; it is a hindrance to their under-

THE NATURE OF GOD

taking any inquiry on the subject, and even to the most spiritual it is the most frequent cause of doubt. The reality on which all depends, with which we ought to be chiefly concerned, is invisible. If God exists, we know for certain that He does not exist as an object that can be seen; He is the one "whom no man hath seen, nor can see." Before this fact is allowed to give rise to doubt, we ought to consider how remarkable it is that, since God is invisible, man should ever have come to conceive the idea of His existence. The visible world presses upon our senses with inescapable insistence; it constantly claims our attention, meets us at every turn, and we cannot close our eyes to it, or for a moment forget it. Beside this tangibility and insistence how intermittent, subtle and unimpressive God seems to be! And yet humanity as a whole has always believed in the existence of the invisible. It might be argued that man has inferred this invisible existence only from certain visible manifestations of it: from ghosts, or from theophanies, that is, from physical or human forms which seemed to be supernatural, of which we have countless legends; from visions seen in prayer, or other exalted states of mind; and particularly, of course, from the appearance of Jesus Christ, held to be the Incarnation of God. But since these sources of the idea are either completely doubted by many people, or recognized to be only symbolic manifestations of God, who remains still invisible; and since even God incarnate in Christ is dependent upon a faith which sees the invisible in Him, and not upon anything that flesh and blood revealed, it is unlikely that any of these things are the causes of belief; in fact, on the contrary, credence has been given to them only because of an already existing belief in God. But the mere invisibility of God ought not to be a cause of doubt. First of all, some of the most important things in the material world are invisible: to begin with the lowest, the air is invisible; light is invisible, save so far as reflected; electricity is invisible until it discharges in a flash; the force of gravitation is invisible. And now visible and tangible matter has been analysed into invisible elements, and we know that the whole of the material world rests upon an invisible basis. Secondly, we ought to remember that things are rendered visible by the fact that they are here and not there, that they are circumscribed and come to an end. Therefore God, who is none of these things, must be invisible by His very nature. If God could become visible to us, we should know one of two things: either that beyond what was visibly revealed He still remained hidden, or that we ourselves had become purely spiritual beings. It is interesting, therefore, to observe that the most overwhelming sense of God that has ever come to man is in intellectual vision, which has no form or visibility whatsoever. Now this negative invisibility of God reveals His nature to be positively spiritual. "God is spirit." Too often spirituality is confused with mere invisibility. There are many invisible things that are not spiritual at all; but we do know of one invisible reality which is spiritual, and that is our own soul or self. The actuating reality which constitutes a man is an invisible one, as invisible to himself as to others. No dissection of his body ever finds it, and for the simple reason that it is not spatial at all. There must be a spirit in man, because no physiological explanation can explain his consciousness; there we pass instantly from a sphere which can be measured and weighed to an entity whose activities escape all such tests. We cannot even *feel* our own souls; we can only infer them from the nature of our thought; still less can we say where in the body the soul dwells. There is an analogy between the presence of the soul in man's body and the presence of God in the world. In any carefully defined sense the soul is no more *in* the body than God is *in* the world; we can only say the body is present to the soul as the world must be present to God. Since, then, we share with God a spiritual being, we know a great deal about God from ourselves; if God is spirit, then we understand something of His nature: it is an invisible, non-spatial activity which is, however, able to act on the visible in space. We can understand how spirit can pervade all things; but we must be careful that we do not image this pervasion as that of a saturating liquid or an all-filling gas. Our minds can travel out to the farthest star and penetrate the mysteries of the atom, not by motion, but by understanding: it is not that the spirit is here or there, in this thing or that, but all things can be *here* to spiritual perception; and spirit can act not only upon and through the physical, but without the physical at all and at a distance without intermediate contact. This is being discovered to be true even of the human spirit, whose attachment to the physical is so intimate and dependent. Thus from the human analogy we can understand and conceive how God is spirit, not only pervading the physical, but beyond it and independent of it. Man is spirit and body; God is pure spirit. This tells us something of the particular nature of God.

The second material from which our knowledge

THE NATURE OF GOD

of God's nature may be obtained is the character of the visible universe. We have seen that the visible, material universe depends upon an invisible and yet still material universe; and this in turn must depend upon invisible spirit. We can gather something of this from the fact that although the visible universe is a reality, it is a reality without meaning save for the mind. We are not considering now in what way the universe depends upon God; that must be deferred for later discussion, but it is obvious that if we can assume that God is in any way the cause of the universe, then from the universe which is the effect we can argue something as to the nature of the cause. And in this connection there are four things that strike us about the visible universe. The first is its vastness. This vastness has become oppressive to our generation through the discoveries made by the telescope, and the calculations of the size of the universe based upon the speed at which light can travel. It is unnecessary to quote the figures which can be found in astronomical works; it is enough to remember that they outstrip all imagination; and yet we must recollect that vast as the universe is, it has actually been measured by the mind of man, and we can use numbers which are approximately correct, even though these numbers can convey nothing to our actual conception. When we say God must be at least as vast as the universe He has created, we must remember the difference between the vastness of physical size and the immensity of spiritual nature. We are not even here arguing from one figure to another, but by pure analogy; the vastness of the universe is only a symbol of the immensity of God, which is not a thing that can be measured by size, but it measures the mind that could conceive and the power that could plan, create and sustain so tremendous a system. For the next thing that strikes us is that it is a system; it is not just a mere amorphous collection of heterogeneous elements; it may look that at first, so much there is, and so many things. But then man's mind begins to discover that it is ruled by what he calls law, though we must be careful how we use that term; it means that things can be classified; that the complexity of life can nevertheless be embraced in a few simple forms; that the multiplicity of happenings can be reduced to a few simple sequences which always follow in the same order; that one thing depends upon another and everything on something else. And here we rise by analogy to some conception of the mind of God: it can hold this vastness together. Since everything all goes back to simple elements which are nevertheless capable of amazing adaptation and amplification, we can conceive some idea of the intellectual power which must belong to God. And when sometimes this vastness overpowers us, and the simplicity of its order looks mechanical, so that we feel everything exists only for the whole, its parts only cogs in a machine, we make a correcting discovery to which this time the microscope has contributed: that the smallest fractions of the universe are as perfectly made as the plan of the whole; in fact, the plan of the vastness is minutely repeated in the smallest particle, so that the atom is found to be a universe in miniature. Moreover, there is a most wonderful diversity even in things that are classifiable under the same heading; no two blades of grass are alike. This immensity and order has not destroyed individuality; so that from this we can rise by analogy to the idea, not only of God's might and God's mind, but of God's care. It takes an interest in the minutest details; it gives to everything an individual stamp. Therefore the parts do not exist merely for the whole; the whole exists just as much for the parts.

The last impression to be gathered from the universe, and the one that comes slowly, and yet with still greater wonder, is the existence of beauty; the sense of satisfaction, pleasure and joy which is given to us by the colour, the form and the proportion of the universe. All this gives us a hint by analogy of something in God that, by its action upon our minds, we can only call blessedness; so that we may know not only that God is might and mind; He is joy and His existence is bliss.

It needs constant interaction between the knowledge which we derive from reflection on our own spirits and the knowledge which we derive from the consideration of the vastness, order, minuteness and beauty of the universe to generate any worthy conception of God. Arguing from our own spirits only, we should feel God was completely knowable, and altogether one of us. But when we look at the world outside we gain some idea of the difference between ourselves and God. These two considerations compel us to conclude not only that God is equal to the world as a cause must be equal to its effect, but that He is something more than the world and something vaster even than the world can reveal.

And now we can go back over these facts and see if we can answer two most important questions which are now emerging: can we discover from our own consciousness that God is (1) personal and (2) moral? Some conceptions of God have risen to

THE NATURE OF GOD

a great height of spirituality and power, but have rejected the idea that God can be personal. Now this is surely due to mere confusion with the limitations of human personality. Human personality is so often arbitrary, unsympathetic, exclusive, individualistic; but these defects, of which we are all conscious as defects, need not be transferred to the personality of God. To conceive God as impersonal would mean that He was without consciousness or character; and that would make Him less than an infant of a few days old. To deny God self-consciousness means to deny Him knowledge; and we are then faced with the alternative of blind force or unconscious will as the cause of things; which takes us back only to physical nature, or to some form of mentality really inconceivable. These conceptions involve nothing but atheism under another name. If the Supreme Being is without consciousness or love, He has no right to the word "supreme." Most people see this on reflection; but it has been maintained that if God is not impersonal, that is something lower than personality, He may be something higher than personality; and this can be admitted if it does not mean that the higher does not contain, but simply obliterates personality. The doctrine of the Trinity solves this problem; for, as a matter of fact, the Christian conception of God does not say much about the personality of God; it does not call God *a person*, but says that He contains personalities absolutely united in a principle; personalities who, so far from excluding one another, are so completely united that they make but one mind and work together as one will, inseparable and interpenetrating. There are not only the obvious defects of our personality which we need not ascribe

THE NATURE OF GOD

to God; we are most of us deficient in personality, for we are not completely conscious. It is held that nine-tenths of our mind works unconsciously; no doubt recent discoveries have exaggerated the value of the unconscious as compared with the conscious mind, for a great deal of the unconscious is merely the relegation to habit of what was once conscious; but it often means that our conscious mind is influenced, sometimes not for good, by the unconscious mind. We are not always master of ourselves; our reason is overwhelmed. All this marks the deficiency of our personality. We can frequently only maintain our personality by assertion, by opposition to others, and we feel we have to fight for our right to express ourselves; we are glad that we can retreat within our own personality where no other can follow us. Then we are conditioned and hampered by the physical world outside and, still more, by our bodies themselves. In all this we are not completely personal. What we, therefore, have to conclude is that God is the *perfect Person*, while we are only *semi-personal*. It is in communion with the personality of God, and, finally, in union with it, that we attain our complete personality.

Again, can we rise from our moral consciousness to a certainty of the goodness of God's nature? If God is only might, and supreme because of that, He is not God in any sense that man can worship Him. If God were not good, He would be no more than the might of nature plus a mind merely cunning or diabolical, and, therefore, morally He would be immeasurably inferior to man. Now, arguing from effect to cause, we must admit that God must be at least as good as man. There is evil in the world, and there is sin in man, and from

THE NATURE OF GOD

this some have argued that what is in the effect must be also in the cause, and therefore we must ascribe both evil and sin to God. These problems will have to wait for consideration later on; but we can content ourselves at this point by saying that man regards the evil in the world as a defect, and sin in himself as rebellion. There is, therefore, no reason for ascribing either evil or sin to God: a cause may be greater than its effects; it cannot be less. Not only must we argue that God is at least as good as the highest man has ever been; He must be more than that, because it is this something more of which man's moral consciousness makes him aware, not only as an interesting fact, but as a constant pressure and call to be himself something higher. And if any man cares to question what he would have to be, even to satisfy his own moral consciousness, he could soon discover that he would have to be perfect; indeed, that there can be no end to his moral attainment. This makes it even more inconceivable that the moral ideal is of his own creation; it is the reality which is seeking to create him; and, therefore, must be referred to an activity other than himself, and an activity transcendently good.

The question then remains whether we can infer that the nature of God is not only spiritual, immense and good, but is perfect, infinite and absolute. It is clear that if God were in any way imperfect, or at least could be discerned by man to be so, then man would have an idea higher than the actuality of God; which we really cannot conceive is possible. God must at least be perfect. It may be that we cannot actually conceive what is meant by perfection, but that does not mean that we may not ascribe this to God quite accurately.

We know by astronomical measurement the size of the universe and the figures may represent fair accuracy, even though they are entirely inconceivable and unimaginable. Can we go further and say that He is infinite? Perfection for us is something that reaches a point where we can say a thing is perfect and can be no more so. What is meant, then, when a thing is said to be infinite? It means that it has no bounds. Now this is obviously again something which we cannot conceive, and yet the moment we give anything a finite end, our thought travels beyond it. Therefore, God must be infinite unless He is going to be something less than our own thought of Him. And for us human beings it means that God is completely inexhaustible, and, therefore, that we can grow for all eternity in the likeness and the knowledge and the experience of Him, and yet never come to that which marks the end beyond which there is nothing more. Our mind admits this, and still more our heart demands it; for nothing but the infinite can satisfy us. It has been held by some thinkers that personality and infinity are irreconcilable. There seems to be no real reason for this; for even the human personality is dominated by the sense of the infinite, which is indeed one of its characteristic marks.

What is meant when it is declared that God is absolute? It means first of all that His being is underived. When we get to God we need go no further, for He is the more than sufficient beginning for all things. While all other things are dependent, He depends on nothing; He Himself is His own explanation and cause; He is self-sufficient. Human thought certainly demands this as the only possible end of its thinking. There is really only one alternative to an Absolute; it is that of an ever-ascending infinite series of beings where there is no one supreme. But apparently no one has ever even dared to try and think that, though some minds have been able to tolerate the idea of an infinitely descending series! But there is no need for this alternative if God Himself be infinite; His perfection involves infinity, and it is His infinity that makes Him absolute.

Since there cannot be two Infinites, there can be nothing beside God and, therefore, His absolute unity is now accepted as beyond further discussion. Anything like polytheism or real dualism has come to be impossible to human thought. But that does raise the question of whether God's absoluteness is meant to be so all-embracing that He is the only reality, and that all else that exists is nothing else but the being of God; that He is the totality of which everything is but a part. If this were accepted, it would involve that all things which seem to have individuality of their own are illusory; but there would then be so much in the world, and still more in ourselves, that would be a delusion that we could really trust nothing else whatsoever. Again, if God is Absolute in the sense that He is the totality of which everything is but a part, the totality ceases to have any reality save as the sum of the parts and, therefore, depends upon its parts, and God is no longer self-existing. And yet, how can we believe that God can have anything else existing beside Himself and yet be absolute? Here we have to try to rise above defects in our thinking derived from superficial considerations. We acknowledge that two *things* cannot occupy the same space; even this is no reason why one personality may not penetrate another without destroying that personality, and God may be able to give a derived and relative existence to other things that does not infringe upon His absoluteness, because that depends not upon blotting other things out and having no room for them, but in overruling them by His greater mind and transcendent goodness. Thus it may be that the transcendent goodness of God remains absolute despite the existence of evil; for He can beget good from evil; and the existence of finite creatures with a real, if relative freedom, need not trench upon His absoluteness, because through their freedom He can win them to a complete oneness of will with Himself.

Thus it seems that from our own consciousness within and from the world outside we can rise with great assurance, not only to belief in the existence of God, but to the conviction that His nature is such that we can trust, love and worship Him, who is, therefore, not only the explanation of all things, but who remains supreme and the guide of all things, and is also the end and eternal satisfaction of ourselves and of all our thoughts. There are thoughts here that touch the mind with solemnity and awe; they do more than that, they remind us that, although we are finite and temporal, we do share in the Divine nature, and that only in union with the Divine nature can we come to the satisfaction of our own being. We must do more than think truly of God, rising from the visible to the invisible, from our own spirits to His; we must by a personal act of will acknowledge not only His supremacy, but His worthy supremacy as our only hope and final anchor. We must further seek to lift ourselves to Him in intimate personal communion, for without Him we are incomplete, miserable and nothing at all.

IV

CREATION

MANKIND, observing the world without and reflecting on its own experience within, has come to a general conclusion that there are three distinct classes of reality: the world of material things; the inner realm of the mind, in the case of humanity functioning through a physical body; and a type of being which is pure mind, and is, therefore, invisible. These three realities are generally known as Nature, the Self, and God. There have always been found individuals who have denied the existence of one or other of these three realities; and in the West, especially in modern times, a considerable number of men have questioned the existence of any mind which does not manifest itself through a physical medium, and therefore have doubted the continued existence of the soul after the death of the body, the existence of such spiritual beings as angels, and, particularly, the existence of God. Before we give too much weight to this particular point of modern doubt, we ought to remember that there are also those who question whether man possesses a mind that is anything more than a highly developed form of matter; while there have been individuals in the West, and there are a great many in the East, who have questioned the reality of the external world. But the majority

CREATION

of mankind agrees in the main in recognizing the existence of these three classes of reality.

When we compare these three realities it is found that man has an immediate consciousness of the world outside, that he only *infers* the existence of the soul, and that he only rises to the idea of God by an argument based upon the reality of both. Theology accepts this position even though it seems to contradict what many may feel to be a fact, namely, that they have an intuitive consciousness of their own soul and an immediate consciousness of God. But introspection will show that it is more strictly true that the soul is conscious than that it is actually conscious of itself. And while the consciousness of God will be claimed by many as immensely strong within them, further thought would have to admit that the consciousness of God is always mediated to the mind. This does not actually place the reality of spiritual things on a more questionable basis than the existence of matter; for when it comes to proving the existence of the world outside us, while few doubt it, probably no one has ever really satisfactorily proved it; and, although no one has to argue that the world exists, since it is immediate to sense, the soul and God must be inferred and argued because they are mental and spiritual realities. At the same time it must be recognized that very few of us are sure of the existence of our souls or believe in the existence of God because of conscious argument; the belief in both seems to have arisen by unconscious mental processes. It is only when we ask for proofs that that process becomes conscious and we can check its working stage by stage. The process is, however, so natural to the mind that the endeavour to prove the non-

CREATION

existence either of the soul or of God can succeed only by questioning the validity of rational argument.

The only form of unbelief which needs to be taken into account is not so much the denial of any one of the three great realities, God, Self or the World, as a subtle effort to reduce two of the three to a mere form of the remaining third. These efforts are generally embodied in philosophical systems with which the ordinary man does not concern himself, and which perhaps the philosophers themselves do not take too seriously. Materialism would make the mind simply a special function of matter, and therefore, of course, give no reality to the mind's idea of God. Unfortunately for this theory, it can likewise give no reality to matter unless there is a mind to perceive it, and, therefore, Materialism is confronted by the opposite theory of Idealism, namely, that mind is the only reality and matter nothing but one of its ideas. But this theory proves equally destructive to mind, since it has to admit that the mind is generally deluded into thinking that the idea of matter corresponds to something outside itself; and this proves that the mind, when taken to be the sole reality, is full of delusions and, therefore, untrustworthy. The third philosophical theory is that known as Pantheism, which strives to make both mind and matter mere modes of God. But while this theory appears at first to make God everything, it nearly always ends by making Him nothing at all, for we have to deny to Him that consciousness which produces in us the delusion that we ourselves exist; and an unconscious God, if it is not merely a high-sounding name for the totality of matter, and, therefore, only concealed materialism, cannot

CREATION

be the only other thing we know, namely a mind, and, therefore, must be nothing at all.

We can leave these speculations to lose themselves in confusion and end up in absurdity, and come to that which is apparent to common sense, namely, the extraordinary difference between mind and matter. This difference it is impossible to exaggerate: matter is that which can be weighed and touched and has solidity and occupies space, while the things of the mind escape all these categories and tests. Even though the mind may be dependent upon matter for its functioning, and although the action of the one upon the other is immediate, and so interwoven that we cannot tell where one begins and the other ends, yet the difference is still unmistakable. Take a solitary instance: here is a piece of matter we call a telegram, certain black marks on pink paper; you can take the totality of these black marks and put them in one order and they mean nothing; you can put them in another order and they spell out to the recipient of the telegram news that puts him into the most violent excitement. That effect is produced wholly through arrangement and interpretation by mind. Yet, while the difference is so extraordinary, there must be some relation between them. And in the end there is no way of accounting for both the difference and the relation save in referring them both to some third reality which has given them their constitution and their relationship for some purpose which the mind ought to be able to discover; that is to say, the difference between mind and matter, and the relationship between them, can only be accounted for by reference to a third reality, namely, God. We shall see, as we go on, how inescapable this argument is, and how the

CREATION

mere difference between mind and matter, and yet the possibility of their acting one upon the other, not only compels us to assume God, but enables us to understand what is God's relation to both mind and matter. It is obvious that God is more of the nature of mind than of matter, since He is invisible. But He must be something higher than mind as we know it in man, because the human mind does not explain the existence of matter or the possibility of contact between them. And also, God must be less dependent upon matter than the human mind is. We know no human mind that is not attached to a body; whereas God must be pure Spirit. In this idea of Spirit we rise to something which makes a real third to matter and mind; though mind must partake of the nature of spirit.

The question now before us is to discover what is the relation of God to both matter and to the human mind, or rather to that which is itself the centre and controller of the mind, the self or soul. Without trying to build up everything from first principles *de novo*, we can save ourselves a lot of time by taking note that human thought in the past has produced three theories to account for the existence of matter in relation to God. One of them is that matter has existed eternally alongside God. But even the eternal existence of matter does not necessarily fix the relationship of God to it. It might be conceived that the world was the body of God, and has therefore been eternally attached to God. But this makes matter necessary to God, and, although the idea is capable of a certain beauty in expression, it will always seem to infringe upon, and derogate from, the pure spirituality of God; it is, moreover, repugnant to religious

CREATION

feeling, because the world as we know it seems less adequate as an instrument for the expression of an eternal Spirit than man's body is for his soul; for it is more fixed in its movement, and, therefore, must confine God in His actions more than man's body confines himself, while it fails to represent at all adequately the ethical nature of God. We shall return shortly to discuss what validity is to be given to dogmatic declarations such as that God is Spirit; and we do not reject the eternal existence of matter simply because it is repugnant to religion, for science seems to confirm this attitude by its discovery that matter is in constant flux and development, which would therefore conflict with the unchangeable perfection of God. The same objection, perhaps, also lies against a second variety of the theory that matter has eternal existence, in which the eternal existence of matter is ascribed to the eternal creation of God; for eternal creation is probably a contradiction in terms. A third variety of the theory of the eternal existence of matter simply supposes that matter has always existed alongside God, but in no sort of connection with Him. This really denies His absoluteness, and even if it were not thought to be a contradiction of His Godhead, since matter, even if eternal, could not be regarded as in the same category as eternal Spirit, yet it would utterly fail to explain how it is that God can mediate Himself through this entirely disconnected and alien reality. It therefore calls for no further discussion.

The second theory of the relationship of God to matter is that the world proceeds from God by *emanation*. This somewhat vague theory is rarely held by minds which have passed through

CREATION

or inherited any continuous mental discipline, for it only seems to have been invented to account for the vast difference between the material world and a spiritual God, by proposing a series of minute changes in which the nature of God itself actually becomes something different. But this would leave the first slight change as incredible and meaningless as the most separate and final difference. Moreover, like the eternal existence of matter, emanationism always presupposes a certain necessity imposed upon God which really derogates from His deity, and generally combines itself with the theory that everything that proceeds forth only returns again by the same law of necessity; which reduces the whole thing to an utterly meaningless movement.

The third theory is that of *Creation*. We are inclined to use this word somewhat carelessly, but when it is put in contrast to the theories already discussed, it becomes clear that Creation means an *absolute* creation, that is, not the mere manipulation of matter into some higher form, but the creation of matter itself. Since we have ruled out emanation, this precludes us from thinking that God created matter out of His own nature, so that it must mean creation out of nothing; which is of course the strict meaning of the word. Now, is this theory conceivable? It should be noted that, like the theory that God is pure Spirit, it is a dogma, that is, it does not seem to be an absolutely necessary deduction from human thought, and, therefore, it comes to be specified as a doctrine of revelation which, by thought alone, man could not have attained. Now, that it is a doctrine of this nature must be admitted. It comes into existence simply as an assertion, no doubt made by men, but claimed

CREATION

as something revealed to their minds apart from their own constructive effort; it is, as it were, an idea which suddenly shoots into the mind, apparently from without, for there is no previous thought to prepare for it.

It is the fashion of modern thought to reject all dogma on principle, and to regard the very idea of revelation as exploded. We must clear this up if we are to approach the question whether creation is a conceivable notion with that freedom from prejudice which will enable us to come to a reasonable conclusion. Revelation is sometimes conceived to be contradictory to reason, which is quite a mistake; but it is often placed in too great a contrast to reason; for it is quite obvious that all reason has to rest eventually upon something outside itself, so that ultimately reason always rests on revelation. The facts of the world are not arrived at by reason; they are there before reason begins; they are the material given to it, and reason neither creates them nor can it alter them. Again, the constitution of mind and the laws by which it works are not its own creation: it has to submit to them to exercise its functions. These two things, the material of reason and the laws of its own working, are prior to reason; though it should be noted that reason can use the facts given to it, they are not alien to it, and it finds its own laws congruous to itself; once they are discerned, it can give reasons for them, though reason itself did not construct them. There is, therefore, no real objection to a thought or idea coming to the mind which is not due to reason; though it must be due to the same source as the facts of nature and the constitution of the mind, that is, to the Creator. But this, only if it is found to be true; its truth, however, established,

CREATION

not through being discovered by the mind or built up from previous convictions, but through being found, when received, to be neither inconsistent with reason nor so entirely unprepared for by previous thought that it does not fit into it, as a key which will open a lock, because the one was made for the other. The doctrines of revelation will be found on the whole to be something like this : they fit into a blank which is left when other theories proposed by the mind have had to be rejected by reason as irrational. Taken alone, a truth of revelation may be very difficult in itself, and may often hold together opposite facts in a way which reason cannot always reconcile, but which it can discern might be possible if its powers were greater. And yet, for reason to reject this one solution would leave the whole problem without any clue at all. We can see the application of this to the particular question before us. We have seen that the theories that matter is an eternal existence, or that it is an emanation from God, are irrational. There is no third theory save creation; so that the theory of creation seems to fill the blank. Our question now is whether this theory is too difficult to conceive as possible.

It will be recognized that man comes very near to creation in his own activities. First, he can so mould the material world that he can vastly change the face of creation. But he has to have material to work upon. He comes still nearer to real creation in the activity of his mind; in its expressions in art he begins with a dependence upon material such as is necessary in architecture and sculpture, but rises to music and literature, in which the use of material is almost dispensed with. By means of this activity man positively builds up a world

CREATION

of his own, through which he expresses ideals of beauty which outstrip nature itself. Amongst his achievements in literature are the creation of characters who, though they have never existed, often seem much more living and real than actual human beings, and often exert as much influence over the course of humanity as living beings themselves. But allowing this to the utmost limit, it is quite obvious that man still depends upon material provided for him, and that even his most fantastic ideas, which have no corresponding existence in nature, can, on analysis, be shown to be simply a new combination of existing things; so that it can be said that man never really creates anything. But man's approach to real creation makes it not inconceivable that to a higher power sheer creation would be possible. We can conceive this most easily in the creation of ideas, and can well understand how God is the Absolute Originator of the thoughts of His own mind. Can we go further and conceive God not only creating ideas, but creating matter?

Now, here again, we only require to push things one stage further. We have discovered that the material world actually consists of various arrangements of a material substrate that itself is invisible. This substrate is supposed by some to be the ether, which, it must be remembered, is a speculative form of matter of the most rarefied type conceivable, not only invisible, but penetrating all things, and, while absolutely solid, able to be penetrated and perfectly frictionless. It is supposed that visible and tangible matter is due to discharges of energy, making as it were knots in the ether. Persons who object to theological ideas, because they are speculative deductions and apparently inconsistent,

CREATION

might well remember that science has to infer the existence of the ether, of which there is no proof, and that it has to assume this contradictory character. But there are some who believe that the ether is nothing but energy. Now, energy cannot even be called matter at all; in fact, we know most about energy as an activity of mind. It is not for a moment suggested that matter can be resolved back into the immaterial, or that matter is nothing else but mind; but there is enough in the scientific analysis of matter to suggest it is not inconceivable that matter is a *creation of Absolute Mind*. Moreover, science itself gets very near to demanding creation: analysis may take us back to a homogeneous material, but no evolution can explain how this material could start changing by its inherent power; for then there would be no reason why it should not have started changing before it did. Since science is bound to assume that this fundamental material goes back to something still more fundamental, eventually it must arrive at the impossible conception that the whole world arose from nothing. That the world was created out of nothing by an eternal Spirit may be difficult, but it is the only alternative to the idea that it emerged by itself from nothing, which is absurd.

Creation, therefore, seems to be demanded by science itself; it looks as if it were only one stage higher than man's own mental powers, and, therefore, it both demands God and can well define Him as the Being who possesses this power of creation. There must be creation, and God alone can create.

But what is creation for? We look out at the vastness of the universe; we discover its enormous power, its wonderful order, the simple unity of its

CREATION

laws; we unroll the story of its evolution step by step until we come to its still more mysterious beginning; and if we assume God made all this, we are bound to ask, What did He make it for? To say that He made it in order to display His power waits on the question: display it to whom? He did not need to display His power to Himself. If we say that God was compelled by some necessity within Himself to create the world, then we are assuming that God needs something beside Himself, and so deny His perfection. If, therefore, the world was not created for His own pleasure or out of necessity, what third alternative is there?

The solution of creation lies in the existence of human beings. It is obvious that all this beauty, glory, vastness and power are unnecessary to God, because He is all these things in Himself, and, therefore, they are wasted until a mind appears that can appreciate them. It is sometimes thought to be a piece of vanity on man's part to think that the universe was made for him. And yet it is not vanity, however much it may minister to his vanity, for the course of evolution has ended in man; it is by man that the universe may be most highly appreciated. It is scientific therefore, as well as religious, to say the universe was made for man; he is both its goal and its clue. But that raises the further question, Then what was man made for? And here we have to take notice of the fact that it is by the method of revelation that the idea has come to us that man, like matter, is originally a creation. It does not matter how much the world has developed; it must go back eventually to creation out of nothing. But it is inconceivable that matter could ever develop into mind; the difference between the two makes that quite impossible. It is not a question of ransacking evolutionary history to find the secret, the secret is closer to us in our own minds; and although we see matter and mind working there in closest proximity and in complete interdependence, yet there is no possibility of regarding the one as of itself passing over into the other. No amount of nerve or brain activity can possibly account for an idea. Therefore, it is not difficult to receive, but a necessity to believe that the soul of man is an immediate creation of God, however the matter which composes his body may have been evolved, and however his mind may develop through culture. But what is man created out of, if not out of matter? It is here that we are tempted without further discussion to say that man is created by God out of God, that is, he is a part of God. But this assumes that God can cut Himself up, as it were, into little pieces; and the idea is not only repugnant, but it is impossible. Personality is a thing which cannot be divided up so that it can become other personalities. To hold that man is part of God is to fall again into the pantheistic idea which only ends up by making either the parts or the whole unreal. We have, therefore, to fall back upon the idea that, like matter, man is an original creation of God out of nothing, only man's spirit is created by God in His likeness; that is, he shares, though in diminished degree, the spiritual attributes of God, particularly in intellect, will and personality.

Now, what is this creature man created for? Here, again, revelation gives the only answer. This creature is created in order that God may communicate to him something of Himself, and this is done by endowing man with certain capaci-

CREATION

ties and desires for God, so that in personal union with God, that is, a union of will and love, man may become a partaker of the Divine nature; there being all the difference between being a part of God and being a partaker of His nature. Now, the moment we accept this dogma of revelation, we shall see that it is reasonable, and that it fits in with everything else; in fact, that it is the only clue to existence there is. We can now understand why material nature was created; it was not only as a basis for the soul of man; God's own spiritual nature needs no such basis, and God could have created perfect spiritual beings. And, indeed, it is believed that such actually exist and are known as angels, creatures whose existence is pure joy, which they live only to express in endless praise and glad service of their Creator. But such creatures, though in a sense much more glorious than man, because of their intellectual power and their purely spiritual nature, must nevertheless remain within their perfection; they can never rise into union with God; they possess the vision of Him; they have boundless joy in Him, but they can never become united to Him. For a creature ever to become united to God, his creation must be of a special character; he must be created imperfect, but with a capacity for rising higher, because union with God is only possible on the free choice of the creature. Therefore he must be created lower than his final intention, so that the final intention, on being revealed to him, may be embraced by him as his own free and glad desire. But in order that such a creature shall not, because of the possession of a lower nature, fail eventually to attain the higher, it is necessary that he should be placed in a world which shall

CREATION

have the power of revealing to him the higher purpose and of educating him for its participation. Therefore he is placed in the closest juxtaposition with the material world; in fact, man is created as a union of body and soul. Hence there is a certain conflict between the desires for the infinite implanted in him and the body with which he is united, while the world in which he finds himself placed breeds dissatisfaction in him, and, indeed, engenders a certain friction. But this pressure and friction of the world serve to keep this dissatisfaction alive and to create in him an ever-growing consciousness that he is made for something higher than what he actually is. The vastness and beauty of the world constantly mediate to his mind the thought of God; the conflict between his spiritual nature and the material world creates in him the desire to be free from this and to rise to a higher state of being.

So we learn that man is created for God in order to share most intimately in His glory and blessedness; that the motive of his creation was not any necessity on the part of God, but pure spontaneous love which desires others to possess what He Himself possesses; and that the rest of the creation is designed to lead man towards this end. It is clear that here we are entirely in the realm of revelation. Man would never have come to this idea by himself, and yet it is, when received, the only clue to his existence. It explains the imperfection of the world. This is not the most perfect of all possible worlds; it is not meant to be; its very imperfection is to prevent man resting in his present condition. On the other hand, its greatness and glory are continually leading man to desire something higher than himself and something

CREATION

beyond this world. And so revelation gives the only true science of the world and the only explanation of existence. Moreover, it explains why the material world has to be in constant motion. It is by the continual movement of things that man's spirit is wakened to realize his own nature: first of all, his difference from the world; and secondly, his dissatisfaction with the world. If nothing ever moved or changed, man would hardly know himself to be alive, and he would not have that desire for eternity and the unchanging which is so characteristic of him. The freedom which is necessary to enable him to choose union with God must be real; and so evolution is necessary in order that man may be continually brought to a place where he can choose the higher. Moreover, since union with God is so glorious an end, it is something for which man as solitary, if not incapable of, is certainly too small to secure any sufficient share, and, therefore, millions of such creatures must be created who, by the interaction of their minds one upon another, increase one another's capacities, and thus their capacity for sharing the glory of God.

If this end of existence should be thought to be too high for man to attain, and this revelation should be rejected because reason staggers under such a prospect, then it only remains to be pointed out that no other end would justify the sufferings and strivings of the human soul through countless ages of existence and in myriads of individual experiences, save that at last man should see the vision and share the blessedness which will make his discipline here more than worth while and will give him a sufficient reason and necessity for eternal existence.

V

EVOLUTION AND THE FALL

EVERYONE who reflects feels that existence stands in need of some explanation. The desire to seek a cause for every effect almost amounts to an intellectual instinct, and the mind of man is never satisfied until it reaches a cause which is sufficient to account for all that exists. The task would be much easier if some of the things that exist could be eliminated, and if we had only to account for mind or only to explain matter; for while it is inconceivable how mind could have developed from matter, it is also not easy to explain why mind should have needed to create matter. It would also be easy to explain existence, if all things seemed to us good; but the presence of evil, pain and sin make the reference of everything to One infinitely good a perpetual problem. If for a moment we take the material side of existence and try to explain that, we may find ourselves nearer a solution, not because material existence explains itself, but because it demands mind both for its explanation and as its originating cause. We shall find that once we have established mind as the original cause, we can understand both the purpose and the method for which the Original Mind brought matter into existence; for we shall discover that there is no other explanation of existence save this: that the Original Mind created matter out of nothing in order that other and dependent minds might be created and brought into true union with the Originating Mind of God.

The difficulties inherent in the philosophical possibility and the religious purpose of such a creation have been previously dealt with. But special difficulties have been raised for the modern mind by the scientific doctrine of evolution.

It is possible that creation and evolution are not contradictory ideas; evolution might conceivably be merely the mode of creation, but before we can decide this we must discover what exactly is meant by evolution. The term itself is ambiguous, the scientific data are in dispute, and whether such evolution as can be shown to have taken place is an explanation of existence or is itself what needs to be explained must be carefully considered.

Evolution may mean the gradual unfolding by an inherent process of something already existing in germ. This is the strict meaning of the word, and if it is to be maintained it entails that the whole mighty universe, with all its varied forms of life, goes back to an original germ of life or form of matter which is a sufficient origin and cause for all that has come out of it and may be further developed in the future. Various suggestions as to how this process might have taken place have been from time to time put forward. It has been thought that the various forms of life may go back to a single cell of protoplasm; that protoplasm can be analysed into chemical elements; and that all these elements can be explained as varying arrangements of something like electric energy; so that, granted the existence of some original form of energy, the whole development of the universe can be explained. Energy begins to move, constitutes the resistance we call matter, by friction sets up nebular incandescence, and gravitates towards a coagulated and revolving centre, which forms a star, and this, by its revolutions, throws off detached masses which become circulating planets, and as these cool to a certain temperature the chemical elements they contain are brought together in a combination which gives rise to organic activity, which develops into vegetable, animal and, finally, human species, with perhaps more wonderful productions still to come. It will be noted that this theory still leaves to be explained the existence of original energy, what caused the change from potential energy to actual movement; for it must have begun some time, and if of itself, there seems no reason why it should not have begun before it did; while it is very difficult to conceive how all that we now see to exist could have been contained in germ and potency in any original form of existence not itself of a mental and spiritual character equal to its final effect. This meaning of evolution is obviously philosophical and speculative, and must submit itself to the criticism of reason, from which it comes out badly; for reason cannot conceive how such a process is self-explanatory. It is a process which gives reason no real sanction, even if it could conceive it, and it is obviously not capable of scientific demonstration. But what is generally meant by evolution is something much more modest, namely, that we can actually detect, over a long period of time, that animal species have been transformed and that the mind of man has amazingly developed. Whether man as a whole can be regarded as a natural development of one of the animal species, whether

EVOLUTION AND THE FALL

all the species can be traced back to one form of organic existence, remains, from the point of view of strict science, quite unproved. We have no examples of widely differing species being transformed from one to another. The chief interest is of course in the possible transformation of animal into human species, but although a few remains have been discovered which some have taken to belong to a creature half ape and half man, such remains are suspiciously few, and their real significance is in hot debate among scientists. It is also remarkable that there should be no living specimens intermediate between the animals and man. Although some existing savage races look like living links, there seems to be evidence that the modern savage has suffered deterioration;. but under the process of education the ape can never be made anything more than a performing animal, while there seems practically no limit, given favourable conditions, to the education of a savage. Modern scientific theories of the descent of man are inclined to regard the existing species of the higher quadrumana and the present races of mankind as collateral rather than as in lineal descent, both going back to some common ancestor. But the divergencies between the species are so great that we may be compelled to push this common ancestry so far back that in the end it will mean nothing more than that man shares with the animals a cellular organism, which nobody of course disputes. The derivation of man's body from the animal world could be accepted if a distinction was made between his body, and even his mind, and his immortal soul or spirit; since the former might be only the instrument of the latter.

It is the theory of natural selection that has

bridged over in thought the actual demonstrable facts of development into a theory of complete evolution without a break from potential energy and undifferentiated matter up through the inorganic and the organic to mankind. But it has to be pointed out, what is often not understood, that natural selection is only a theory of how evolution has come to be, and that it is now recognized that it must be largely a negative factor and cannot of itself account for evolution. Granted that it is characteristic of all life to produce constant, though slight, variations, and that, on account of the struggle for existence involved through the over-productivity of the species, the variations bringing advantage in the struggle for survival tend to survive, it remains obvious that the real cause of evolution is variation. Moreover, it is difficult to see how slight variations, when they first occurred, would bring any advantage, and so why those who possess them should survive and transmit them, and these slight variations should go on increasing until they bring some advantage. It is also difficult to see why the whole process should have led to a mental and finally moral development, as it looks very much as if in the mere struggle for existence strength would always have told, and man with his physical weakness and need for protection, and with the handicap of a growing conscience, would never have emerged under any such process. Even if such progress could as a matter of fact be traced, the process would still need to be explained. Modern science is compelled to grant more importance to the inherent variability and the upward tendency of life than to natural selection; so that on purely scientific grounds there remains no explanation for selection.

EVOLUTION AND THE FALL

That like should produce like and things should remain always the same is more rationally explicable, but that life should develop ever upwards really needs as much explanation as if water should be found running uphill.

In the presence of these facts and in the growing difficulties of the conception, while it cannot be doubted that some evolution has taken place, there is less disposition to extend it to the whole of existence, and there seems a necessity to hold: either that there has been intervention at such points as the creation of energy, the beginning of movement, the appearance of life and the emergence of any creature that could be rightly called man; or that energy, inorganic matter, organic life and the main divisions of animal existence, as well as the human species, have developed side by side from totally different starting-points.

It would be dangerous, however, to build belief in God or the supremacy of spirit upon any such arguments. The issue stands more like this: there are a great many objections, from a purely scientific point of view, to the theory that man has directly descended first from the animal and then from the inorganic; and those who wish to take advantage of these difficulties and to reject the theory of absolute evolution are perfectly justified in doing so. It is questionable, however, not only whether this is wise from a religious point of view, but whether it is even necessary. All that a Christian theology demands is either that God must have originally endowed nature with the powers which have led to its evolution, or that evolution itself is nothing but a display of the constant creative activity of God. If matter is to be conceived as inherently possessing all the

EVOLUTION AND THE FALL

potentiality of life, then we are conceiving something quite different from what is ordinarily implied by the term "matter," and are employing ideas which involve mind, and approximate rather to the conception of God. The idea of evolution and creation have been already brought together in the title of Bergson's book, *Creative Evolution*, and we have only to reverse the phrase to Evolutionary Creation to suggest a conception to which Christian philosophy has no objection. Evolution then becomes simply the Creator's method, and it is simply a question to be decided by scientific fact whether this is His method, and whether the process has been worked from one starting-point of unbroken development from the atom to the brain of man, whether there were a number of starting-points, or again, whether there have been interventions by the invasion of a new gift from above. Theology asks science to observe no other limitations than that theories should not be allowed to outrun facts, and that scientific philosophies should not involve the impossible theory that everything has come from nothing, put forward explanations that explain nothing, or ask us to believe that the totality of all which at present exists has always existed germinally, and has developed in such a fashion that it needs no further explanation of spirit, mind or creative power.

But there is another difficulty involved in the acceptance of the evolutionary hypothesis, and that is that it seems in complete contradiction to the traditional Christian doctrine of the Fall. On the one hand we have the theory of a continual and unbroken rise, a real ascent of man, while on the other we have the belief that man has fallen. Although at first sight it looks unlikely, it is possible that both theories may be correct; the one may explain the development of his body, the other the condition of his soul. But if they are to be reconciled, we must take a wider view of the whole situation, and be careful that we do not press either evolutionary hypothesis or the doctrine of the Fall beyond what is actually demanded. Now it should be noted that the doctrine that man has fallen is not only a doctrine of revelation; a similar idea is found in the mythology of many primitive peoples. Moreover, this mythology must owe its rise to a conviction of man that something has gone wrong with his own inner life. He finds there an amazing and painful contradiction and a curious conflict: high ideals and noble aspirations which he constantly falls beneath, and sometimes denies and rejects. It is very doubtful if that internal contradiction can be explained by any evolutionary hypothesis. It has been supposed that the sense of contradiction might be explained by man's animal inheritance: the instincts of the brute remain within him, and these offer resistance to, or at least act as a drag upon, his higher nature. But it has to be pointed out that the sins of which man accuses himself and the guilt which he feels cannot be explained by this means. The sins which disfigure human nature are not mere animalisms; the animals obey the laws of their own nature on the whole far better than man: they know when they have had enough to eat, their sexual instincts do not lead to enslaving excess or to unnatural perversions. These faults are found only in man and, strangely enough, in the domestic animals which have been brought into closer contact with man. It is not even possible to trace the sins of civilized man to the

EVOLUTION AND THE FALL

survivals in him of savage customs or explain them as the "herd instinct" overcoming his conscientious convictions, for many of the most flagrant evils of civilization are due to man's loss of a social consciousness, in short, to his unbalanced individualism, which leads him to act not only against the welfare of the whole, but also on the assumption that other people will not act in the same foolish way as he does, since otherwise society would come to an end. When the sense of sin comes to clear consciousness, it is the sense of having seen a higher vision and having turned away from it. Evolution alone cannot explain this. On the other hand, we must be careful not to read into the doctrine of the Fall extreme theories in the other direction. First of all, it should be noted that the expression "the Fall" does not occur in Scripture. It is obvious also that the story in the early chapters of Genesis, from which the doctrine of the Fall is derived, is a highly symbolic representation of something which must have had a historic beginning, but which perhaps could not be conveyed to the mind as history; for that might involve covering a vast track of history and time, telling in detail an endless series of individual experiences. It is clear that the plucking of the fruit of a tree would never give anybody knowledge of good and evil; we are here entirely in the realm of symbol. How far this symbolism extends it may be difficult to determine; some would hold that we must retain the idea that Adam and Eve are historic individuals, the ancestors of all mankind, who together sinned; others, taking the very name "Adam," which is only the Hebrew for "man," and the fact that Cain fears to meet other men and goes out to found a city, feel that

EVOLUTION AND THE FALL

this cannot be regarded as a story dealing with individuals at all. All that we need to retain is that the symbolic story must be concerned at some point with an individual choice which carried with it consequences for the whole race. But it is also clear that since we are presented with a creature who does not know the difference between good and evil, we may be in the realm of moral innocence, but we are forbidden to think of a perfect human creature already endowed with a fully developed consciousness like that possessed by modern man. Again, Catholic theology stands for a much more reasonable and restrained doctrine of the Fall than that which has often been popularly understood. The Fall has sometimes been explained as taking place from a position of high perfection, and of leading to such deprivation that fallen man is left without sufficient reason to lead him to God and with such an utter weakening of will that without supernatural grace he is unable to do any good. The Catholic doctrine is that man as created was given the help of supernatural grace, which, however, was no essential part of his nature, and that by his disobedience to Divine command he was deprived of this supernatural grace and left to the working of his own nature until such time as his own need led him to cry for redemption, which redemption was offered to him in Christ; but not merely so that he should be restored to his original status, but that by grace he should be elevated to an entirely new position in which his actual nature is transformed so that he becomes a partaker of the Divine nature. Now within the bounds of this at first sight somewhat curious and complicated theology there is undoubtedly room for the scientific theory of evolution, as also for a sane estimate of the actual condition of human nature as we now know it. It must be remembered first of all that no fall is conceivable until man has arrived, by whatever evolutionary process, at a state where he becomes conscious of God and can be made an offer which his knowledge and sense of responsibility enable him to choose. What is offered to man at this stage is communion with God, made possible by supernatural grace. What man seems to have done is to have rejected this offer and endeavoured by his own powers to rise to a Divine life, snatching at what was offered to him, desiring to take it in his own way and to use it for his own purposes. He preferred the knowledge of good and evil before life, he sought to satisfy curiosity rather than to attain to moral power. Thus man sought to rise, but by a wrong route; the result is he has been allowed to retain all that he grasped; the knowledge of good and evil he does possess, but the knowledge does not of itself guarantee his choosing the good or refusing the evil; in fact, he is constantly choosing the evil even with the clearest knowledge that it is evil, and that its consequences will bring him suffering and shame. We can therefore retain the idea that man has risen, as well as the idea that he has fallen. He has risen intellectually, but he has fallen morally. The ancient story, thus interpreted by the light of evolutionary theory and Catholic theology, is seen to be remarkably true to the actual condition of humanity. Man has made enormous intellectual advances; he has gained vast knowledge of the secrets of nature; he has invented countless means of harnessing nature to his own purposes; and all these things, intellectual power, knowledge, invention, are in themselves good; but every one of them has been perverted because man's moral character has not equalled his knowledge or vision.

This interpretation of the Fall seems to be equally true of man's history, so far as we can recover it. When we get back to real primitive man, he is extraordinarily chaste and wise, even though it is on a purely instinctive basis. But with the first touch of intellectual awakening or social development everything seems to go wrong; he abandons his instincts, and for a time has nothing to put in their place, and with this his primitive restraints are broken down and his salutary customs turned into horrible and cruel perversions. This does not mean that it would have been better if man had never abandoned instinct for intellect, or that he ought to have remained in his original social system; but that alongside his rise there has also been a fall, which has always corrupted and diverted all progress, and not until intellect and instinct can be wedded together again and man's individual consciousness can be reconciled with a higher social communism does there seem any hope for his redemption. The redemption offered to him by the Christian religion is not, as we have seen, a mere restoration, but it is an exaltation above anything for which man's nature was originally fitted: he is now called to something even higher than communion, namely, union with God; and for this there has to take place a new creation. The old one having failed, the remedy is a new creation on a much higher level; the very working out of man's folly leading him at last to see the need for this and to accept it as the only way of redemption from the miseries into which he has fallen.

EVOLUTION AND THE FALL

There are, however, difficulties remaining even with this interpretation of the Fall. As we look back upon history, we are appalled by the long story of man's upward struggle, seeing that it has had to take place in such darkness and ignorance. This difficulty has been intensified by the picture of primitive man presented to us by anthropology, and especially by the enormous extension of time demanded by evolutionary science in order to account for the development of man to his present position. Within the Biblical perspective, which is variously calculated to begin the history of man four thousand or, at most, five thousand years before Christ, it was once possible to feel that this was perhaps only adequate to work out the divine purpose; but from various arguments built on the development of man's language and the acquirement of the arts, his remains found embedded in geological strata, and the time calculated to allow the human species to have developed from an animal ancestry, various epochs extending from ten thousand to a million years have been demanded for human history. The awful slowness of the process and the millenniums of darkness and misery involved seem to make it unthinkable that God should have used such a method, or if those methods were necessary, have dared to contemplate what creation involved. But the picture of the past must not be reconstructed under the assumption that it entailed a million years of misery before light or hope began to dawn for man. It must be remembered that many of the sketches of primitive man with which we are presented in popular outlines of human history are highly speculative. We know very little of what primitive man felt or thought; there are only two things

EVOLUTION AND THE FALL

about his interior life that we know with any degree of certainty: one is that he had extraordinary artistic gifts which themselves bespeak an experience of joy; secondly, he had strong religious beliefs that this life was not the end of all. In endeavouring to picture primitive man we must remember that so long as man's ancestors were actually animals, the religious problem does not emerge; for the animal is a happy creature. Whether there was a stage in which man was half animal and half man, a stage marked by intense misery, when man was struggling for light and finding it not, we do not know; indeed, it is impossible for us to conceive what such a stage could mean. We are compelled to say any creature is either animal or man, and can never be half and half. We must also avoid contrasting primitive man, however we conceive him, with civilized man, and too hastily assuming that because the former did not have our knowledge and possess our inventions he was therefore more miserable than we are; there is plenty of evidence to the contrary. Not only does primitive man present no more difficulties to the Creator's goodness than the condition of savages to-day, but he does not present quite so many difficulties as civilized man, who seems to have burdened himself with misery and lost nearly all the consolations of faith. It has to be remembered, moreover, that the vast stretches of time over which the process of evolution is believed to have extended do not really increase the pressure of the problem. Even if we could find a human being deeply conscious of religious need, seeking something, he knows not what, and with all revelation and grace denied him, the multiplication of millions of such cases would not correspondingly multiply the problem. It is a psychological fallacy to add up vast tracks of time and to multiply individual experiences, for it must be remembered that a man's consciousness is his own alone, and there is no mind which can total all consciousness save that of God. In this sense each man lives to himself, so that we cannot even say that man has existed for millenniums; man has never existed in this sense for longer than any human being has lived, and really not as long as that, for our own consciousness is almost wholly taken up with the present. Moreover, it is very much to be questioned whether any man who cries out after God in any desperation does not at last find Him. The awakening of religious need and the answer of Divine grace are not only nearly simultaneous; it must be the touch of the Divine that first awakens conscious need of God.

There is a remaining question, however, and it is whether God ought to have created man with a nature that was liable to fall. It must be answered that unless man had within him the choice and power to rise or fall he would not have been man; and it is only when he reaches such a stage that he can be properly so called. But this does not completely answer the question. We may wonder whether, if man must be created capable of being brought into union with God, and that must depend on his choice, so that there must be the possibility of refusal; and whether, since God must have foreseen man would refuse, for such the doctrine of omniscience probably demands, it was not taking too great a risk for God to create man at all? It would have been so if He did not possess within Himself the power of Redemption,

EVOLUTION AND THE FALL

so that, whatever happened, all contingencies were already provided for in the wisdom, power and love of God. Moreover, the Fall of man seems to hold out the hope that the possibility of evil, which must always theoretically remain if freedom is to be real, will now be so finally worked out that it will never become actual again; for the consequences of evil are such that in time even man learns from them, and then turns to accept God's higher way. If there are other orders of being, and if we believe that there is another life than this, the Fall carries with it the hope of redemption for all worlds and the guarantee against any further Fall, and even if we could total man's miseries on earth, they would be absolutely insignificant beside the glory and blessedness that redemption opens up for man. Therefore, providing we can assume Creation, the Fall and Redemption, evolution may not only be reconciled with them, but be regarded as the method of the Creation and the means of bringing man to a position where, even if he falls through attempting a mistaken way of exaltation, that fall only makes possible a redemption which goes beyond the furthest demand of evolution, revealing its purpose to be that of lifting man from sheer non-existence to share the nature and glory of God.

VI

HUMAN FREEDOM AND RESPONSIBILITY

MAN in his present condition is a strange and bewildering mixture. It does not matter whether we look upon man in the mass from without or investigate our own selves. Man is capable of rising to great heights of goodness, nobility and saintliness, and of sinking to dreadful depths of depravity and malice. And not only are some men good and others bad; the same man is sometimes good and sometimes bad. At all times self-examination will show that a man is partly good and partly bad, and very often he is conscious of a tremendous struggle going on within between good impulses and evil desires. The very motives by which we act, we can discern by close analysis to be very mixed. A good deed may be done from bad motives, and even when our motives are of the highest, we can often detect in them an admixture of selfishness, the desire for human praise and the mere seeking of reward. This mixed condition of human nature is one that evidently stands in need of some explanation, and there are only two theories which hold out any hope of explaining man's condition. The one is that he has evolved from inorganic nature and inherits from an animal ancestry, and that

HUMAN FREEDOM AND RESPONSIBILITY

because his evolution is incomplete there is retained still within him the dead drag of physical nature, limiting and hindering the aspirations of his soul, while there are still present within him animal instincts and primitive savage habits which constantly tempt him to surrender his present attainment, which strive against his conscience and sense of social duty, and which frequently bring about his fall. The other theory is the theological doctrine that man is a fallen creature, that he has introduced this discord into his own nature by sin, that is, by deliberately disobeying his conscience and going against his better judgment.

We have seen previously that the scientific doctrine of evolution and the theological doctrine of the Fall, if they are both carefully defined and kept within their respective spheres, may both be true, and need not be in complete contradiction. But this defining of their respective territory entails that evolution has little or no bearing upon the question of sin, and therefore does not account for the conflicting elements in man's nature. Even if we took evolution in its most absolute form and accepted the idea that the soul of man was nothing more than a further development of feeling, instinct and consciousness, it would be difficult to understand how this higher development of man, by hypothesis entirely derived by natural processes from its physical and mental antecedents, could, by its mere emergence, bring about such a stage of conflict. The sudden insertion of a soul of great spiritual capacity into a body evolved from animal forms and retaining its animal instincts would indeed offer a readier explanation of man's condition, or at least make the conflict more understandable. But, as a matter of fact, any close examination of man's

HUMAN FREEDOM AND RESPONSIBILITY

actual condition gives us very little reason to believe that his condition is due to any form of evolution, whether absolute or relative; for man's chief and deadliest sins are not those which have anything to do with his physical nature, but belong entirely to the invisible and spiritual part of him, for they are selfishness and pride. Moreover, even judged from man's present highest moral attainment, neither the animals nor savage peoples sin as he does. The animals are not more cruel than man can be, and the instincts and appetites, which are so often blamed as the source of our temptation and the cause of our depravity, are not found in the animals in excess or perverseness. Primitive man, so far as we can judge, or even surviving savage races, when uncontaminated by contact with civilisation, are free from many of modern man's most disfiguring social crimes and are not so flagrantly self-seeking. The idea that man has introduced a conflict into his nature by an act of rebellion and a deliberate choice of evil seems to correspond much more closely with his actual feeling and judgment concerning his own condition. This feeling is one of regret, failure, something once had and remembered, now lost; a sense of sin, a feeling of guilt, an accusation of folly is not only expressed in all our literature, it might almost be said to be the creator of all our great literature, giving it its tragic quality, its poignancy, its sadness. The same thing is evidenced with equal strength in our common conversation. We are always thrilled by a noble act, but we are never surprised by it: we are constantly amazed at treachery and astonished at baseness. Although most men are liars, at least sometimes, we always appear to be newly surprised when anybody tells us a lie. The sins of man are an ancient story now, and they are monotonously the same, but they are always news. And if we dared to investigate and weigh our own inner feelings, we are all too well aware of the remorse and self-loathing into which we can fall when we contemplate the things that we have done and the unalterable fact that it was we who did them. All this seems much more consonant with the theory that man has fallen than with the theory that he is gradually rising. In addition, it is most curious that although all men have fallen, and there is no one who is not conscious of sin in some form or other, this universal fact is one to which we refuse to settle down. We all feel that we ought to be different, and the prospect that we may yet do better and rise higher is never dimmed by the fact that we have so often failed, for the hope of doing better is almost constant, even with the worst of us. What troubles us more is that no amount of doing better wipes out the fact that we have done so badly. Here again the idea of a fall seems a far better explanation of our feelings than the idea of evolution. Nor can it be said that this is due to the doctrine of the Fall having so long ruled human thought, and that now, when the doctrine of evolution has been applied to explain man's present moral condition, we are ceasing to feel this. Indeed, it can be said that as our consciousness is being developed under modern psychological discussions the sense of interior misery threatens to become only the more intense, despite the fact that some recent psychological theories have boldly advocated the evolution of man's moral consciousness as the sufficient explanation of his condition of conflict and feeling of guilt.

We must be careful, however, that we do not take the theological doctrine of the Fall to be

HUMAN FREEDOM AND RESPONSIBILITY

identical with some of the popular misunderstandings derived from it, which sometimes have attempted to describe the condition from which man fell in terms not only not necessitated by Scripture, but in considerable contradiction to it; but more especially these misunderstandings have often taken far too pessimistic a view of the condition in which the Fall has left man, making him out to be utterly depraved and incapable of any good. The Catholic doctrine is that the Fall has deprived man of neither knowledge nor freedom, although it may have dimmed the one and limited the other. The most important of all the effects of the Fall to be considered is whether and how far this has still left man a free and therefore responsible being. The question of human freedom is one of the most difficult to discuss; not because it is difficult to believe, but because it is so difficult to state. Determinism has been said to have all philosophy on its side and all common sense against it. That man possesses freedom is extraordinarily difficult to prove, but nearly all action and thought is undertaken on the hypothesis that it is true. This should not entirely surprise us, because to claim that man is free claims that he is, in some degree at least, an originating cause, that is, that in this respect he is ultimate; therefore all efforts at explaining freedom are bound to have the effect of appearing to explain it away. It is one of those things which has to be assumed; but unless we are willing to assume it, all discussion soon comes to an end. It is not surprising that it should be more difficult to define than its opposite; for it is something that can be easier felt than defined; in fact, the feeling of it is its chief witness and its very essence. It is the undoubted verdict of man's reflective consciousness that he himself

HUMAN FREEDOM AND RESPONSIBILITY

has the power of choice, that he is constantly exercising it, and that for the exercise of this choice he is responsible. It is not only the inevitable conclusion of his thought; thought itself is a process in which choice is always being exercised, and is meaningless unless thought is free. It has been said that this feeling ought to be disregarded, because it nevertheless cannot be rationally justified; but if so, it is difficult to see what else in life can be regarded as fundamentally sure. It has been claimed that if a stone which had been thrown by someone could feel, it would feel that it was throwing itself, and therefore that man's feeling that he is free is of no more value. The truth is exactly the opposite, for if a man were thrown down, say from a building, he would feel anything but that he was doing this himself. Man is conscious that sometimes he is being carried away against his will. Such occasions when man is conscious that he is not free cannot be used as an argument that he is never free; on the contrary, they would never even be brought forward were it not that they are distinguished from other acts which are free. When a man knows he is not free, as when, for instance, he is under the influence of alcohol or some drug, he recognises this because it is not his normal condition. It would be just as logical to dismiss this as unreliable feeling, as his ordinary consciousness of freedom. The very struggle which sometimes take place between influences within a man is again a witness to his freedom; he would feel no struggle if he were not free to go in this direction rather than in that. Again, man's reproach of himself and of his fellows for having taken the action that he did and not some other, would be quite meaningless and mistaken unless it had been possible for something

HUMAN FREEDOM AND RESPONSIBILITY

different to have been done. Human society is organised on the basis that man is responsible; and responsibility must be retained for quite other purposes than attaching blame or inflicting punishment; it would be impossible to organise society or run life on any other basis. Perhaps what is most impressive is that the adoption of a thoroughly deterministic philosophy would make complete nonsense of all human thought and life. If, for instance, as in recent psychological theories, it is suggested that all our efforts at rational thought are really dictated by unseen motives which have no claim to be considered as rational, the tables can be neatly turned on this type of argument by inquiring whether these same psychological theories are not also determined by hidden motives and instincts, and, therefore, whether they are of any value at all. If man were not free to choose how he would act, we should not only have to refrain from accusing him of folly or weakness in doing wrong, we should not even be able to exhort him to do good, because he would not be free to change his direction because of our advice. It is therefore instructive and confirming that Catholic theology here comes down on the side of common sense, as indeed it always does, and declares that the Fall has not taken away the freedom which belongs to human nature. Man is still responsible; he knows better, he ought to do better, and he can. And therein it also comes down on the side of our higher human hopes, for without this fundamental conviction, the belief in progress, which is so strong in our times, would be proved baseless; unless man is free he can never be reformed, and with belief in his freedom gone, all hope for mankind would be lost. What would be the value of the constant demand for liberty

HUMAN FREEDOM AND RESPONSIBILITY

which so stirs our generation unless man was able to be free? Fortunately, whatever doctrines men accept, they go on believing in freedom. But it is only Catholic theology that can justify our common-sense and practical belief on this issue.

It is more difficult, however, to state positively the facts about human freedom so as not to raise objections to it. Difficulties about human freedom are often raised unnecessarily because the doctrine is often expressed in an absolute fashion that is easy to attack and bears no relation at all to actual facts. It is not to be claimed, for instance, that man is absolutely free, that is, that every man can always at any moment do anything that he likes. It cannot be denied that many of our acts are habitual and do not come up for any decision at all. There is no need to deny that very often a man may decide, but be unable to carry out his decision. A man may act in freedom and yet in such a way as to barter away his freedom and bring himself into a condition of slavery. It is perfectly obvious that no man is free to be and to do anything whatsoever; he is free only to be and to do within certain prescribed limits, namely, those which belong to the possibilities of his nature. All that need be maintained is that there are times when his choice is free, and that even within the possibilities of his own nature there is always open to him a large area of free decision. It must also be remembered that it only needs a very small element of freedom to make an enormous difference, and that it does not matter in how few things freedom of choice is given; as long as there are one or two, this will make all the difference. Even if sometimes man is unable to carry out the choice on which he has decided, it is the fact that he is able to choose at all which constitutes the main issue. Catholic theology does hold that the Fall has greatly weakened man's will so that he often cannot do the things he would, but it also holds that he can still discern the good and desire it, and even if he fails to carry this desire into attainment, this element of freedom must lead him to strive, and to seek the help which will enable him to attain.

The difficulty about defining what is meant by freedom lies in this, that when we get back to any act of free choice it seems impossible to decide why one thing is chosen rather than the other without making the reason for the choice its determinating cause. If between two alternatives there is no motive why one is chosen rather than the other, then the choice seems to be purely capricious and of no moral value at all; whereas if the strongest motive determines, this seems to prevent real freedom of choice. First of all, it must be replied, what gives any motive its weight is ourselves, and it is therefore our own self that decides. It is not indeterminism which constitutes freedom, but self-determination. Even this, however, presents certain difficulties, for the self must act according to its character, which has been built up from its own past decisions. And so any element of real freedom still seems to belong only to a choice of which no rational account can be given. The only escape from this dilemma is to be found in Catholic theology, which does not need to define freedom in this useless indeterminate sense. Man is only free when he acts in accordance with his nature. Now according to Catholic theology man's nature was created good and his natural tendency is to desire the good; but this is not allowed to be a complete determination; man can so use his freedom as to go against his nature and to choose not good, but evil. Now this is an abuse of freedom, not only because, as a matter of fact, it involves losing his freedom, but also because in thus acting he is not acting in accordance with his nature. Man's freedom is therefore really found in following the tendency of his nature and in choosing the supreme good, which is the glory and service of God, which indeed is his perfect freedom. Man can nevertheless choose otherwise, for he could never have done so if he had not been given the power to do this; and this choice had to be given him, otherwise goodness would not have been his own choice, and would therefore never have been real goodness at all.

We have now to ask the final question, Then why did man choose evil? and the answer is, We simply do not know. There can be no answer to that question, because it was an irrational act. It is here that we arrive at a conception of man as an originating cause, but unfortunately as the originator of sin. It is that which is the capricious act, that which has lost him the true exercise of his freedom; he has used his power of choice, which ought to have led to the choice of good, to the creation of a new thing, sin. This almost looks as if the conclusion were that man is free, but unfortunately so. But we must not argue that it was his freedom which made him choose sin; he need not have done it. This conclusion is one that is very abhorrent to philosophy, for the simple reason that it is a fact which cannot be explained; it is the breaking into the world of sheer irrationality. But we are not to let its abhorrence to philosophy prevent us from accepting a fact which cannot be explained, for there is one element of hope bound up with this conclusion. It was the misuse of a good thing that brought sin, the misuse of the gift of freedom; this misuse was originated by man. This brings a double consolation: first, that sin is a creation within time by the dependent creature man; second, that it is a perversion of something that is good. For the alternative that all other conclusions would lead to is that sin is eternal and necessary, and if it is, we can never get rid of it. So while sin does place upon man the responsibility of being its creator, it carries with it by that very fact a certain hope, or at least possibility, of redemption. That this is a true account of how sin came to be is confirmed by the fact that sin is seen always to be a perversion of something. It is not enough to say that sin is a merely negative thing; it is more than that. But on the other hand it is not a thing in itself, but the perversion of something else, and that in itself good. Hence this abuse of freedom does not lead to freedom, but to slavery. This may be seen also from the way sin develops. Sin arises by man turning away from the ground and goal of his being, which is God; then, since man must have something to worship, he immediately sets himself up in its place. From this proceed pride and in turn all the other deadly sins: first his mind rebelling against his self-worshipping soul, then his body rebelling against his mind, then his fellows rebelling against him; the misery of our minds, the enslavement into which our passions bring us, and the social anarchy of mankind being thus traceable to sin. But here again, the more it deepens man's guilt, the more it holds out hope that if man could be welcomed back by God and simply make His glory once again his sole aim, everything in life would be put right.

There is another question, however, now to be faced. How far is mankind as a whole responsible

HUMAN FREEDOM AND RESPONSIBILITY

for sin? No one any longer quarrels with the doctrine that original sin is transmitted to the whole human race: and this is not only by personal heredity, but by social heredity or environment. A man inherits, instead of a tendency towards good, a tendency towards evil. In addition, the constant example of sin in the world is not only a perpetual temptation, but a continual suggestion. How can it be held that mankind as a whole now living is responsible for sin? Nobody can claim that anyone living now is personally responsible for original sin, and in some sense, though with lesser certainty, we even say no one is responsible for all the sin that he commits, because much of this may be due to inherited tendency and social influence. It looks, indeed, as if, instead of blaming man now living for original sin, we have to blame the ancestor of the human race for all the sin that has since followed. But we must be careful that in reducing responsibility to its right proportions we do not take it away altogether: for that would be an absurd conclusion. The first man who sinned is not responsible for all the sins of the world, for the inheritance of original sin has not entirely taken away man's freedom. And the influence of social sin is not similar to infection by disease; it can be resisted. It is sometimes argued that in a mystical sense we are all members of one another, so that we do share in one another's sins, because it is our common human nature that sins and not merely the individual. Hence we are accustomed to the feeling of shame when anyone sins, because we feel that in some sense we have sinned with him. But while this may be true when we are considering mankind as a whole, it cannot make any man personally responsible for sins which he does not individually commit, and therefore we

HUMAN FREEDOM AND RESPONSIBILITY

have to say that man is not personally responsible for original sin. And, indeed, Catholic theology admits that original sin can only be called sin in a secondary sense, for in the strictest sense sin must be a voluntary, and therefore an individual, act.

Man's responsibility rests on quite other grounds, and is accurately apportioned to the exact amount of freedom that he at any moment possesses. Now, although we can never tell how much freedom a man possesses, we can always tell how little he possesses; the least freedom a man always possesses is freedom of choice, the freedom to know and to choose the good. This element of freedom is enough to make him responsible, and we can determine from this, not how much he is responsible, but for what he is responsible For it does not matter for the moment if, although man chooses the good, resolves upon it and wills to do it, he finds himself, however inexplicably, doing the evil. This, no doubt, frequently happens, and therefore it is not within the power of anyone to apportion the exact responsibility that anyone else has for the wrong he does. It is not always possible for anyone accurately to determine this in his own case. That does not mean that we can conclude that a man is never and not at all responsible; that would make all human life meaningless and hopeless. But his responsibility lies precisely here, that when he knows he ought to do the good and does not do it, or when he chooses to do the good and somehow he finds he cannot carry out his own will, then he must be aware that he is in a very dangerous and desperate condition. The conflict and outcry in his own nature soon tell him that. When he finds himself in that condition he ought to cry to God for help. Man is not respon-

HUMAN FREEDOM AND RESPONSIBILITY

sible for being in a condition which has been caused by original sin, but he is responsible for not getting out of that condition. What, however, man seems to prefer to do is to try to get away from himself, to forget what his condition actually is, and to repress the conflict in his own mind and think of something else. Here he seems to act with the same folly and caprice to which alone we can trace original sin. It is for this neglect, and not merely for what is derived from original sin, that man is held to be responsible, and it is for this neglect alone that anyone will ever be lost. Thus the responsibility for sin is in Catholic theology nowhere carried beyond the facts. It does not wait upon a subtle discussion about whether a man is free, nor upon a decision as to the degree of his responsibility. Man may not be free, but he is able to be free, and that is his responsibility.

But there is something that makes the whole matter still clearer. As we have seen previously in discussing the Fall, man attempted to snatch at the glory of God so that he might say he had obtained it by his own efforts and held it by his own power. Now when he did that, God had to take away from him the capacity to do anything of the kind, for if he could have succeeded, a disaster ten thousand times more tragic than that which sin has caused would have been effected: man would have secured the power of God without having the character of God; in short, he would have become a devil. Now man could not be created already sharing the glory of God, for the glory of God could not be bestowed upon a creature; it must be something that a man chooses for himself, since goodness is only goodness if it is a matter of choice. But the actual capacity for the glory of God was lent to man, so that if he chose it, it

HUMAN FREEDOM AND RESPONSIBILITY

could be his. But when he snatched at it, seeking to gain it on wrong terms, and hold it as if it were his own creation, this capacity was taken from him. Nevertheless, the yearning for God was never taken from man, nor was it possible for his nature, created with this as its end, to be satisfied with anything less. So man's constant yearning for God, and his misery without Him, remains; in addition to this, his own inability to do the thing that he would, to carry out his own choice, makes him incessantly aware of his condition. These two things create a tremendous incentive for man to cry to God to redeem him from his present intolerable position. The Christian religion promises redemption to those who thus call upon God, since He will forgive if they repent; that is, if they will admit the wrongness of their choice, their responsibility for remaining in their present condition, abandon their false ambitions and make God alone their glory. Then the power of the Atonement wrought by Christ will lift man to become united with God after such a fashion that he can never fall again, because he has now freely chosen goodness and for ever, and thus has become united with God's holy will, and so is made a partaker of the divine nature. God has therefore used the fact of the Fall to lift man to a still higher condition than that for which he was originally intended, to make what was a mere capacity an actual and eternal attainment, and has thus secured that even with that freedom which man now shares with God he shall never use it for any other purpose than to be one with Him for ever.

We therefore have to conclude that the modern discussion of freedom has been confused, first of all by regarding man as absolutely free, which he is not, and then by regarding any loss of freedom

HUMAN FREEDOM AND RESPONSIBILITY

as equivalent to being without freedom altogether; for man only needs to possess the tiniest fraction of freedom to have sufficient to make him utterly and eternally free, if only this freedom is rightly used; for his true freedom does not consist in being able to choose anything whatsoever, but in being able to choose that which God intended that he should choose. Man's present condition is a loss of absolute freedom in two respects: he has so used his freedom as largely to destroy it, and the condition into which he has thus fallen has left him with very little freedom indeed; but the freedom which is left, the freedom of choice, which does not necessarily carry with it the capacity for carrying out his choice, demands that he should choose the good, and if he does he will be driven to call upon the help of God to enable him to attain it, since he cannot attain it by himself. To choose not to do this is where the personal guilt of sin alone ever rests. It has to be admitted also that many of our acts are quite irresponsible, but responsibility is something that man can rise to and ought to assume. In one sense we may say man is not responsible; that is what is the matter with him; he is irresponsible; he is trying to get away from his own nature. Man is striving to sink even beneath what he is, but the yearning of his own nature for the end for which he is created makes that impossible; and all the conflict and failure and misery of life only work out to compel him to seek to recover his freedom, which he can only do as he resolves to use his nature for the end for which it was intended, and seek the help of God's grace, by which he can be forgiven, redeemed and restored to live in harmony with the will of God, his highest good, his only perfection and his everlasting bliss.

VII

PROVIDENCE AND GRACE

THE creation of all things by God, as an absolute act in time, by which things that previously had no existence are brought into being, is a doctrine which certainly demands much thought; but it is in turn demanded by thought. Although Creation is a doctrine of revelation, once revealed it is acceptable to reason because reason is unable to discover any other origin for existence. But the doctrine of Creation entails another doctrine as its supplement, namely, the doctrine of Providence; which means, not only that God provides for the needs of His creation, or that He sees the end from the beginning, as the term generally connotes, but specifically, that He guides all things to the end which He has purposed. If the doctrine of Creation is the final explanation of how things that now exist came to be, the doctrine of Providence is the final explanation of how things as they now are shall attain their end. It is, therefore, a doctrine which mainly concerns man and is proposed as the ultimate explanation of history.

Providence is not a doctrine solely dependent upon revelation, for it has been constantly deduced from the observation of history and from individual experience, even by the heathen; and the fact that it is constantly used in modern times as a pious substitute for the name of God shows that even when under the pressure of modern scepticism men have grown doubtful about the existence of a personal God, they are still driven to believe in some all-controlling overruling power. But the doctrine of Providence as deduced from natural observation is heightened by revelation, when it declares that providence secures that end of all things which God intended, and works out, not only in regard to the whole, and when measured over vast spaces of time, but penetrates to the details of all life and provides every single soul with what is best for it; for this latter is certainly not to be deduced from observation, but is based upon faith.

The conception of Providence may be used to include the whole activity of God directed towards His creation subsequent to the creative act, and is then taken to mean the perpetual power which sustains the universe and provides man with everything necessary to life and salvation. This wider use of the word raises an interesting question, namely, whether the material and physical elements of the universe were originally endowed with the momentum which perpetuates their existence, so that all things proceed according to their original intention and impetus without further interference, guidance or help; or whether, in addition to the creative act, there is needed the sustaining power of God in order to keep things in existence, an activity which could not be intermitted for a moment without everything ceasing to be; and also whether things develop according to an inherent impulse originally bestowed upon them, or need to have

PROVIDENCE AND GRACE

exercised upon them an educative power by which new forms of life are developed from pre-existing forms. For it is open to question whether, on a basis of pure physics, the forces of the universe can be regarded as self-sustaining or are perpetually replenished from invisible sources; as it is also open to question whether, on a basis of pure biology, the variations which appear and the transformations which take place under the process of evolution can really be explained by the mere existence of their antecedents, or whether they presuppose the working of fresh creative power. A decision on this issue lies with science, and whichever way it goes it is immaterial to theology. Some would feel it a more wonderful exhibition of divine power to endow all things originally with the forces that make their evolution possible; while others would welcome the idea of the perpetual activity of God as alone accounting for the continued existence of things and the development of life. Some would welcome the original endowment theory because it would seem to entail a more rigidly ordered universe, while others would prefer the continuous creative theory as leaving more room for freedom. But theology could not accept the notion that an order planned by God left no room for freedom, or that a series of perpetually fresh initiations would not still reveal the order of His mind. On the whole, therefore, it is better to keep to the more precise definitions of theological science, which, to the act of creation, adds the perpetual operation of God's "conservation," so that the continued existence of the universe does depend immediately upon His will; and further distinguishes by the term "concurrence" the power provided by God, which man may use for his own ends; but prefers to reserve "providence" to indicate God's overruling of the free acts of man, so that they serve the end which God intended. God can endow things with inherent force, and animals with instinct, which makes them perfectly carry out the Creator's intention. But with the advent of man and the choice made possible by his intelligence and the gift of freedom, providence must come into operation if the end proposed is not to be missed or frustrated; for providence secures that the same end will be attained whichever road is taken, that man will only carry out the will of God, however much he rebels against it, and that the glory of God will be attained even if man himself loses it.

The doctrine of Providence therefore involves something even more wonderful than the doctrine of Creation. It must allow freedom to man and yet maintain the sovereignty of God, make possible the weaving of a perfect pattern out of the chaos and disorder which man in his blindness and rebellion may produce, give to every man the power to do as he wills and yet secure that the will of God shall prevail. It must bring good out of evil and make evil intentions serve a good end. Providence must therefore work without the slightest coercion of man's will, externally or internally. The gift of freedom to man is not a mere illusion which enables him to imagine that he is doing things while really it is only God doing them; for God explicitly dissociates Himself from man's sinful acts. Neither does God govern man's conscious designs by an unconscious purpose, somewhat in the way in which modern psychologists believe man's conscious mind to be really governed by his subconscious desires. The action of providence is rather to be likened to a very skilful chess-player who, whatever move his opponent makes, will always reply with another that defeats his opponent's object and carries out the plan he has all along intended to a successful issue, using his opponent's moves as an aid rather than finding them a hindrance. This presumes the infinite wisdom of God and His perfect patience.

Now, however difficult it may be to conceive in detail how this providence works it is easier to discuss providence at work in human history than it is to deduce creation from the existence of the universe; for the action of providence has been discerned by many thinkers who have not known or accepted the Christian revelation. Even to-day, when belief in the creation of the world and the guidance of mankind by a personal God is widely rejected or felt to be impossible, belief in the inevitable progress of humanity and in all things working out in the end for good maintains itself in a most remarkable fashion. The belief in providence must therefore be due in some measure to actual observation.

The most notable example of providence overruling events is to be seen in the way in which God has used the Fall of man to further man's redemption. For it is held that the Christian redemption is not a mere corrective of the Fall or a mere countermove to man's rebellion, but that God actually uses the Fall to bring about salvation. God had purposed to bestow upon man a supernatural boon, and this could of course have been done without man falling into sin; but when the Fall took place, then God used its consequences to make man cry out for salvation. And although the Incarnation might have had to take place, even if man had never fallen, as essential to his perfection, the Incarnation would not have entailed the tragedy of the Cross; but since it has, the Cross has been made the very means of reconciling man to God and lifting him up, through the penitence it produces and the grace it generates, to the supernatural destiny for which God had created him.

Outside this greatest of all examples other activities of God's providence can be discerned operating within the natural sphere. The actual progress of humanity, mental, social and moral, must be admitted from the study of history; however much may have to be subtracted from the too optimistic, undeviating and inevitable conceptions of progress which have become almost a fetish of the modern mind. But as we read the story of that progress, see how slow it was, how constantly it seemed set back by the break-up of social order, the overthrow of kingdoms, the decline of nations, the decay of culture, what fears concerning and desperate resistance to progress have had to be overcome, almost everyone is compelled to postulate some power outside man as necessary to account for progress. Human progress is not a self-explained process, but is itself one of the manifestations of providence. What from an enlightened point of view we are compelled to regard as the great racial and social sins of polygamy, slavery, war and economic exploitation can nevertheless be seen to have contributed something to progress, and this has often been made an excuse for their being retained when man's conscience at last wakens to condemn them. But a more careful analysis shows that what they have contributed has been by an overruling of their evil rather than by anything inherent in institutions, practices and customs which are now coming under ethical condemnation. Very frequently also superstitions, in themselves baseless and mistaken, can be discerned as embodying and protecting certain social and ethical interests of humanity, until the same interests can be replaced by reason and conscience. Such are the superstitions which have been expressed in the fears of blood, sexual taboos, the sacredness of royal persons; for they have helped to stay man's hand from bloodshed, to control his passions and to engender a respect for social order, even though the ideas which acted as a protection we now know to have been entirely mistaken. Finally, the errors into which man has fallen concerning the nature of God and the meaning of religion, which are embodied in heathen rites and doctrines, have, despite their gross perversion of the truth, kept man in mind of the unseen world and the need of recognizing a higher order of being than himself. Some of the governing conceptions in the great world religions have served as preparations for the reception of Christianity, either by the need they have voiced, but which it alone could satisfy, or by the ideas which they have expressed in myth, but which Christianity embodied in a historic person. Similarly, the definition and enrichment of Christian doctrine owes its very emergence and necessity to the rise of heresies, against which the orthodox faith had to be formulated in a more definite fashion and on a more assured basis. Thus we see providence turning man's rebellion, ignorance and error to the service of social progress, ethics and religion. This working of providence is comparable to the working of instinct in the animal world, where creatures perform the most wonderful acts for the benefit of the species, of which they can have no prevision or understanding.

The working of providence becomes still more manifest when man begins to study his own past and to discern the lessons that he is meant to learn. He sees how a selfish, tyrannical and exclusive social policy has brought nations to misery and their kingdoms to destruction. The discipline of a nation through the events and lessons of history is illustrated in unmistakable fashion in the history of Israel, where there were combined mighty happenings and an inspired interpretation of their meaning. This particular line of supernatural illumination through history was not, however, due to favouritism, but precisely so that humanity could the sooner learn the meaning of God's dealings with all peoples. So also the constant rebellion of Israel against the divine guidance and call, and the tragedy of its rejection, remain to influence the world both as a warning and as an ideal. Again, the great catastrophes which have overtaken humanity, which in themselves seem nothing but unmitigated evil, as plague, famine, storm, flood and earthquake, have taught humanity the need of sanitation, interdependence, and foresight, as well as the need of planning life with reference to an eternal horizon, and of living it on the understanding that at any moment it may end.

There falls here to be considered the question of particular as distinguished from general providence. We can discern providence guiding masses of men over vast areas of history, but does this extend to embrace the events of individual life? It has been a constant belief of pious persons, especially on looking back over their lives, that they have been wonderfully guided, preserved and helped. Many people have been converted to religious faith by some event which they have felt compelled to regard as a special intervention of Providence on their behalf, and many people, as they grow older, come to a more believing and trustful view concerning life, because they can see how it actually works out in their own case when long views are taken. In the very nature of things it is difficult to decide the question whether any particular event is a manifestation of providential intervention. It would be foolish and impious to deny that God can and does intervene to save or guide or illuminate individuals; but it would be equally impossible to reduce particular providence to a general law, or even to decide whether any event was actually a special act of God on our behalf. Certainty on this point would lead men to expect intervention where it would be very bad for them, and wherever such is believed in, it must always remain a matter of individual conviction; and especially ought its occurrence never to be traced to favouritism, but to some wider purpose of God. What it is safer to affirm is that God's general providence does work out to what is best for each individual, and can, especially with their co-operation, overrule everything to serve the highest end; and that particular providence, where it can be established, must always be regarded as manifesting general providence, since it must be intended for the benefit of all. This point will have to be dealt with further when we come to consider the question of prayer and miracles.

The general purpose of providence is to bring every man to a position where he recognises the need of coming into personal relationship with God. The general tendency of the historical process is to bring man to an individual consciousness, and, at the same time, to awaken him to the need of personal religion. In the education of nations, as well as in that of individuals, this process will seem slow, and often it will be marked by the awakening of a religious sense which seems concerned almost solely with the selfish idea of getting God on our side, whether by that we mean our nation, our tribe, our family or our individual selves. But the very endeavour to do this is itself educative, and brings man at last to the point where he sees that his real need is not to get God on his side, but for him to be on God's side; not to pull God down to his level, but himself to be raised to accept the will and to know the mind of God. Providence leads man to recognise his need of grace, and it is here that a general process passes over into a particular purpose.

Grace must be defined as the supernatural help given to the individual in order to enable him to attain to the salvation purposed by God. Grace is thus providence individualised. The study of the creation shows man the necessity for believing in God; the study of providence in history teaches him that he ought to take up an attitude of response towards God's love and care; but the endeavour to make such a response reveals to man his weak and sinful condition, and therefore his need of grace. Grace is the richest term in Christian theology; it is used to describe the spontaneity of God's attitude towards us, and its independence of any merit or attraction on our side. As such it covers the whole of God's relationship to us. There was no necessity in the first place for God to create us; that was an act of pure grace. God did not owe it to man to make him capable of union with Himself, that is, to lift man above his natural level to a supernatural state of being. Still less does God owe it to man, when he rejects His purpose, chooses otherwise and falls under the slavery of selfishness and sin, to redeem him, to persuade him back to the truth and to undertake the task of his sanctification. As man comes to know and judge himself, he finds he has no merit in his own eyes, and knows therefore he can have none in the eyes of God. As he comes to learn the meaning of God's dealing and the cost of His forgiveness, he is overwhelmed by the patience and concern of God spent on one so unworthy; for he can give to God no adequate response for His love and no real reward for his redemption. While grace is used to define the attitude of God towards us, on which our salvation depends, the impartation of His own nature, which is both the means and the end of our salvation, is through all its processes and phases also called grace. Therefore grace has to be distinguished: firstly, as God's permanent attitude towards us, which is that of a will to our salvation, and therefore includes a willingness to forgive us for our condition of rebellion and sin; and secondly, as the actual power which enables us to respond to God's attitude and which brings His purpose to effect. These two meanings of grace, which we may distinguish as the objective and the subjective, can be discerned as distinct and yet inseparable in all God's dealings with us. For instance: grace may be distinguished as *universal* and *particular*, as *sufficient* and *efficient*, as *prevenient* and *co-operant*. Universal grace is that which is bestowed on all mankind, and is sufficient to enable every man to be aware of his need as a sinner, and acts prior to, and alone makes possible, any response that he can make. Grace becomes particular when any man, admitting his need, turns to God in repentance and faith; for then grace becomes efficient to bring him into a state of salvation, and thereafter is constantly co-operant with all his aspirations and resolutions, until it becomes what is called sanctifying grace, actually making him a saved soul according to the eternal purpose of God.

It is concerning the need of particular grace that there seems to be so much misunderstanding, and concerning universal grace that there seems so much doubt. Universal grace is the grace given to all men; for inasmuch as God wills the salvation of all men, He must provide the means to salvation, which are sufficient illumination and power to enable them to know their condition and cry for help. It is believed that this grace is truly universal, operating for instance, not only in Christendom where the Gospel is known, but in the heathen world; as we can now discern in a more charitable estimate of their religions as containing true enlightenment and administering real comfort; so that we are driven to conclude the heathen will never be lost merely through ignorance, but only, as is also the case of those who have known the Gospel, through disobeying their conscience and rejecting what light they have. But in order to bring all men to an acknowledgment of their need, there is a perpetual pressure of providence directed towards this end. One of God's ways of persuading man to admit his need is by writing out the story of his personal sin in magnified and arresting characters in the disorders of society which sin creates. He sees there how his carelessness brings suffering upon others and upon future generations; how his avarice multiplies itself into an order which makes cruel injustice one of its inevitable results; how his fear of his fellows and lack of faith in spiritual power leads to the vast defences which precipitate war and make it even more horrible and extensive. God works again to bring men to a knowledge of their need by the spread of culture; for as men become more self-conscious and can commit their inner thoughts and feelings to writing, they voice ever more clearly and poignantly the unrest of their hearts, and testify to the complete failure of anything apart from God to bring satisfaction and peace. The literature of self-revelation provides overwhelming evidence that neither in selfishness nor pleasure, neither in the pursuit of learning nor in absorption in work, neither in the enjoyment of nature's beauty nor in love of one's fellows, whether of an individual or of humanity as a whole, is there found anything to satisfy the heart of man; only in one direction is there the slightest evidence that there is even the promise of peace, and that is in union with God. Providence is everywhere working to bring man to recognise his need of grace, despite the fact that so many seem quite careless about religion and unconcerned about their souls. The widespread existence of this attitude at the present time is probably a temporary phase in between the acceptance of religion as a convention and its discovery as a personal necessity. But the striking and unexpected conversions, the growth of boredom and depression, the swift and intolerable depressions that swoop down upon all sorts and conditions of men, whether they have attained or failed, whether they are rich or poor, whether they have many interests or none, are an indication that when man at last gets down to himself, his delusions stripped bare and his self-erected barriers overthrown, he knows his need of grace; and all social pressure, mental progress and personal experience are forcing man to this knowledge.

The grace which alone can save a man's soul is an entirely supernatural gift; it could be nothing else, because it is intended to lift man from a life of nature to the life of God. Therefore man can do nothing to win this by his own efforts; he can only receive it as a gift from God. But man is not left merely to wait for salvation as if it were a question on the one hand of God's arbitrary action or, on the other, of His bringing a soul into being as if by a new creation. As a natural creature, man is endowed with the desire for God, and not even his rebellion or his choice of false gods can do anything to satisfy this desire, which remains despite all his efforts. His natural condition is therefore due to "sufficient" grace, but its intention is to bring him to a condition where he wakens to the need of "efficient" grace. What brings a man to that condition depends upon his use of the grace already given. But even if he makes such use of it that it brings him to a position where supernatural grace can now be bestowed, even this is not to be regarded as meritorious, and thus as *winning* further grace, because it consists in nothing else but facing and admitting the fact of his natural condition and his unsatisfied need in that condition; and there is no merit in admitting the truth.

Christianity is the meeting-place of providence and grace; for it is the supreme example of God's providence, because all history prepares for the Incarnation and through it there is revealed to man his actual destiny, which is that of being made a co-heir with Christ and a partaker in the divine nature. Christianity is also the means by which grace is the more directly brought home to the individual person by the manifestation, through the death of Christ on the cross, of a love which embraces the worst of sinners and is not turned aside even by the sinner's desire to destroy the appeal of love in the attempt to murder the Son of God. The appeal of Christ, as incarnate and crucified Love, bears upon man with such pressure as almost to coerce him, leaving him only the very fragment of freedom, lest his acceptance of Christ's perfect grace should not be his own act. The Christian revelation is therefore the ultimate working-out of divine providence, bringing man to a point where to reject the proffered salvation is to bring down upon himself utter condemnation.

The consideration of the responsibility in which the Christian revelation involves all that come within its reach helps to remove any sense of unfairness in the particular incidence of that revelation and its slow spread among the nations of the world. We have seen that grace is given to the heathen, and to those who do right and serve God according to their light there is given salvation according to their capacity; therefore, while the acceptance of Christianity lifts that salvation on to an immensely higher level and increases the capacity of the soul in order that it may partake more deeply of the glory of God, which is indeed capable of infinite degree, yet it at the same time intensely increases the responsibility of those who under its illumination do really comprehend the salvation which is offered to them. In that responsibility there is embraced the duty of making this salvation known to all mankind, which, if wilfully neglected, either by refusing a personal call or general opportunity, would seriously diminish the chance of that soul's salvation. While those living under the sound of the Gospel and within the reach of the ordinances of grace are capable of a degree of sanctification which the heathen cannot attain, they are in much greater peril of damnation through having seen the light and rejected it. And yet this increased responsibility cannot be pleaded as an excuse for leaving the heathen in their natural condition, because, while the knowledge of the Gospel does not guarantee and coerce conversion, even if it increases the measure of loss and the merit of damnation if it should be rejected, it at the same time immensely decreases the likelihood of its rejection. Thus the whole movement of our age, which is bringing the world into closer contact, is part of the working of providence by which God is seeking to bring all men to a more perfect knowledge of Himself and to press upon every living soul the inestimable gift of saving grace.

VIII

THE PROBLEM OF EVIL

IF all existence is to be traced ultimately to the free creation of an infinitely wise, powerful and holy God, how are we to account for the presence of evil? This is the age-long problem presented to human reflection, and especially in our own times proves the most serious obstacle to faith, many people to-day declining to accept the idea of God as presented by Christian theology because they regard it as irreconcilable with the existence of evil. The first thing to be done in considering this problem is to take it seriously; nothing is to be gained by making light of it. Secondly, it must be recognized that what makes the problem so heavy is precisely the view of God set forth by Christian theology. This view does not allow us the relief of believing that there are two ultimate, opposed principles of good and evil, as Zoroastrianism taught, which, however, no thought-out system can sanction. Neither can we posit alongside God, as some modern thinkers have done, the eternity of matter, presenting in itself inherent difficulties to the Creator which could not be entirely overcome, so that existence only displays the best that mind could do, working on the lower principle of matter; for, as we have seen, matter itself must be traced to the free creative power of God. Nor, finally, can we take refuge in the idea that God is lacking in power or is finite, as some modern opinion is inclined to affirm, although God's omnipotence must not be taken to mean that anything whatsoever that can occur to the human mind must be possible to God: nothing is possible to God which is inconsistent with His own nature; but this only involves the limitation of mere power by wisdom, goodness and love, so that God can do nothing foolish, evil or cruel. This is not really a limitation of power; it only corrects the false conceptions of power by which human thought is sometimes confused. It is the idea that the universe is not a necessary existence, but is entirely due to the mind of God, which creates and intensifies this problem, for in so many respects the universe not only falls short of His mind as revealed by other means, but seems to contradict it. We do not demand that the material universe should give a complete revelation of God: material existence could never give a complete revelation of a person; only a person could do that; indeed, no person could give a complete revelation of God save God Himself. But we ought to be able to demand that the material creation should not contain anything opposed to the wisdom, love and power of God.

Neither, in another direction, can we take advantage of the theories which propose to regard evil as non-existent and due only to a delusion of the human mind, though we are at liberty to refer modern pessimism to their existence as indicative of its exaggeration. There is a certain amount of truth in such theories, for it must be remembered that evil is only a subjective interpretation of the human mind, and is liable not only to exaggeration and misunderstanding, but to pure delusion. Even the most popular of these theories, namely, that pain is all due to mortal mind, has in it a considerable element of truth, for pain is a sensation of the mind, and apart from the mind would not exist. Moreover, we know that the mind can feel pain which has no cause outside itself. But to hold the theory that *all* pain is a sheer invention of mortal mind, and has no objective cause outside the mind, is contrary to all common sense and physiological observation, and, even if true, would still make the existence of mortal mind the greatest of evils, since it imagines the pain that plagues it.

Nor is there much relief in the suggestion that evil is really nothing, but a mere privation of good, as theologians ever since St. Augustine have maintained. This may be true enough, and the truth is always of value, but it hardly relieves our problem. Of course, evil is not a thing in itself; it is a mere attribute of a thing. Moreover, we are bound to believe that everything in itself, since it was created by God, is good, only something has happened to turn its effect into evil; but this is surely something more than a mere privation, it is a positive perversion.

It has been a more common device with modern philosophical thought to regard evil as due to the incomplete and short-sighted view of things which man is bound to take; whereas, seen as a whole, and with regard to its end, everything would appear good. It is only because the pattern is unknown, and its working out is hidden from our mind; to the mind of God all things must appear perfect and good, and if we could only rise to the mind of God, we should see things after the same fashion. But this is a very doubtful and dangerous explanation: it means that man has only to attain a right view of things, he need not attempt to change anything. This is contrary to all the instincts and aspirations of humanity, which feels that there is evil in the world which calls for radical change. Can we believe, for instance, that human sin and the suffering which it causes are only evil to our point of view, and not to the mind of God? As man grows more like God he becomes more conscious of the evil in the world, not less.

It is, however, quite open to dispute whether the extent and depth of the evil is so great as has been imagined. For instance, there is no doubt that the problem of evil presses heavier upon our generation because of the modern consciousness and fear of pain. It is more than likely that the development of the individual consciousness under modern education and civilization has increased the sensitiveness to pain, and that man cannot bear pain quite so well as once he could. The quickening of the powers of imagination have added to actual pain the pain which is suffered by its anticipation, which is often even worse than the actual pain turns out to be. Thus it has come to pass that, to the modern attitude, pain is the worst of all evils; but herein it is mistaken. The increased sensitiveness to pain may be welcomed as not only inevitable but valuable, for pain is the outcry of health and strength against the invasion of disease and danger. The suffering it entails compels men to seek for remedies, and for remedies which not merely take pain away, but remove its cause, for it is the disease and not the pain which is the danger. We can therefore look for the lightening of our problem at this point, for not only will advancing knowledge be able to decrease physical and even much mental pain, but we have the right to expect a moral growth in men that will not be so paralysed by the fear of what pain may still remain.

There is no doubt also that the extent of the evil in the world is magnified by the fact that more of it is now brought to our knowledge. Nevertheless, it must be remembered that there is no more suffering in the world than at any moment any one person can feel. The idea that we can take everything that people have suffered at different times, or all the suffering that at any one moment different people are feeling, and add this together, is a psychological fallacy. The consideration of this undoubted fact diminishes the magnitude of the problem and prevents us from coming to the conclusion, as some have done, that existence is nothing but suffering, or, ar least, that there is a balance of suffering over pleasure. There can only be one consciousness in which suffering may really be totalled, and that is the consciousness of God. At the same time it makes for the elevation of the human race, not only in nobility and sympathy, but in practical benefit through the efforts to relieve pain, the more man approximates to the mind of God. Wider sympathy with pain must therefore be welcomed, but it must not lead to the false conclusion, which often tends to paralysis and despair, that the totality of the suffering we can feel is an objective reality.

Again, the extent of evil is magnified by the unfolding of the story of evolution which, if some calculations be true, extends the history of sentient life on this planet to perhaps a million years or more, and compels us to weigh the fact of animal suffering which, even when we think we can discern some purpose in human suffering, seems quite purposeless. But not only is this suffering exaggerated by the psychological fallacy to which we have already drawn attention, but it is questionable whether the animals ever suffer in the same way that man does. We must hesitate to say a word that would not only seem to sanction callousness, but might diminish the all too lamentably deficient sense of our duty to refrain from inflicting pain upon the animal world; but the mere fact that animals cannot anticipate pain as man can must make an enormous difference; they may have a memory of pain as man has, but, as in his case, memory cannot actually reproduce physical pain. The picture of "nature red in tooth and claw," because some animal species prey upon others, has been considerably overdrawn; the animals which are killed by other animals or by man for food do not suffer what they might suffer by lingering disease, which in the animal world is almost unknown. The interesting fact common to all these three forms of delusive magnification is that the growth of subjective consciousness is valuable as leading to the diminution of actual suffering, but is misleading if taken as an index to the extent or depth of objective suffering. There is the valuable hint here that to be willing to suffer pain is one of the surest ways to its removal; so that these considerations both decrease the weight of our problem and help towards its entire removal. Nevertheless, after all these deductions have been made, a mass of evil does remain, and it is a question whether mere diminution does anything towards a solution of the problem. One solitary evil in a world made by an all-wise and all-loving God would still be a problem.

The problem therefore remains; the only question is whether it is so great as to inhibit faith in the existence of God, arrived at by man's use of his reason and argued from his moral consciousness. The dilemma involved must be faced to its ultimate conclusion. If there were no God, and if the existence of the world could be explained without reference to Him, then the problem would have vanished, even though the fact of evil still remained; for in a world which originated without mind or feeling, but in which both afterwards emerged, evil could only be expected, for mind and feeling would be confronted by an alien order which was not even prepared for their emergence, and, therefore, the moment consciousness arrived suffering would begin. Moreover, the more consciousness developed, the more suffering would be bound to develop, and even if all physical pain were removed, the mental pain of man, confronted by a mindless and meaningless universe, would be intensified. The whole human race would at last be engulfed in despair, and would, as a logical conclusion, plan its own extinction as the only way of relief. But not only is it impossible to explain the emergence of mind on any such hypothesis, while it would explain the existence of evil, it would now make the existence of good a problem. Why man should ever have any pleasure or happiness at all would now need explanation; in fact happiness, wherever found, would be due to a lack of feeling or forethought, and, therefore, would be an offence to reason; happiness would become something which ought not to be. Along this line there is no solution, and the effect of its exploration and widespread acceptance by modern thought in the pessimism that it produces is an additional confirmation that it must be all wrong. Therefore, we have to look in the only other direction, and are bound to accept the idea of God as infinitely good, wise and powerful, and the Creator of all that exists, and then either

THE PROBLEM OF EVIL

confess that the existence of evil is a problem which we cannot reconcile, but must leave trustfully in the hands of God, or try still further to see whether the presence of evil in God's world cannot be explained without at the same time explaining it away.

The explanation that Christian theology would advance is that evil is an intrusion into the world which God has created, due to the actions of dependent, but free personalities, and chief among these is the evil wrought by the Fall. There can be no doubt that a vast amount of suffering in this world is caused by " man's inhumanity to man " ; if only we could eliminate the moral evil of which man is the author, this world would be a much more tolerable and beautiful place. Lust, avarice, cruelty and selfishness are responsible for much that man suffers. Apart from what is traceable directly to human sin, a great deal of suffering is attributable to carelessness and ignorance, but there is no doubt that if man's mind were only free from its moral perversions there would be let loose such a flood of illumination, such a dedication of all knowledge to human welfare, amelioration and kindness that the world would soon become a very different place. Even when man suffers from himself and not from the evil wrought by his fellows, as through fear, worry and mental conflict, this again is largely due to his false values, his wrong moral attitude, his lack of trust in spiritual realities. It is now believed that the agonies suffered by the mentally deranged might have been prevented not only if there had been available mental therapeutic skill, but in many cases if also the beginnings of anger, suspicion and egotism had been checked in time.

There is a view of evolution which would remove from man all responsibility for evil, by regarding him as possessing a mind and a moral consciousness which has gradually developed and is only now awakening to itself; and if this is the whole story, then all suffering is traceable to human ignorance, and, therefore, to the Creator who determined that this kind of evolution was the best way by which the education and emergence of man might be brought about. But it is very questionable whether this theory of evolution is historically true, or at least is the whole truth, or that most of man's suffering can be traced to ignorance. There are many evidences of deterioration not due to ignorance, but to man's unwillingness to accept, to face and to follow the truth he knows and to make it known to others. With all our modern advance in knowledge we see that this does not necessarily bring with it a corresponding moral improvement. Marvellous discoveries of nature are applied not for the healing and help of mankind, but more often for its destruction and hindrance; it has been said that the invention of machinery, which ought to have relieved man of so much drudgery, has done really nothing to lighten or shorten his labour, because its advantage has been almost entirely appropriated for creating wealth for the few and further enslaving the many. Since we have ample proof in this age of widespread education that knowledge is not virtue, it can no longer be claimed that sin is nothing but ignorance. The theory of Christian theology, that it is sin which is the cause of human suffering and sorrow, is not only borne out by many facts of history and observation, but rightly interpreted is a more hopeful theory; for if we have to ascribe evil to God, the Creator, then man is never likely to get rid of it. But if the Ultimate Cause of all things is Perfect Goodness, and evil is only due to some secondary principle, such as the free will of a dependent person, then we have indeed some hope that goodness may ultimately prevail, and sin, being unnatural to man, may be wiped out. Whereas if goodness only emerges with man, it is a new and alien thing in the universe, and has little chance of imposing itself upon a scheme framed without reference to moral ends, or of ever conquering man's own nature which inherits instincts and impulses which were shaped under non-moral conditions, and, despite all emergent intellect and idealism, will continue to dominate his life through the insatiable desires of the flesh and the influence of the unconscious mind.

But even if we accept the theory that much of the evil that man suffers is ultimately to be traced to the Fall, it is difficult to refer to this event, however interpreted, the sufferings borne by animals through their preying upon one another, and the sufferings inflicted upon man by such natural evils as volcanic eruptions, earthquakes, storm, flood, intolerable heat and cold and the failure of crops. It may be that animal suffering has been immensely exaggerated, and that natural evils would take less toll of man if life were better organized and laziness did not make people prefer to live in danger zones where life is easier, instead of in the parts where it is safer though harder. However diminished, there does remain a large amount of evil which cannot be referred to any sin or carelessness on the part of man. And in order to account for this residuum, Christian theology, working upon hints in the Scriptures, posits a further malevolent influence due to beings of a higher grade than that of man, though still dependent upon God, who have also fallen, and since from a higher altitude, into a profounder perversion than man himself has even been able to reach, leaving no trace of good whatsoever, but only a nature consisting entirely of envy, diabolical malice and implacable hostility. There can be no doubt that the Scriptures, although only in obscure hints, and without a complete revelation of the cause of, or the possibility of redemption from, such a fall, do contain references to the agency of demonic powers, and that on the greatest of authority; for it cannot be questioned that Christ believed in the existence of evil spirits, who are not only the cause of many of the evils which afflict mankind, but are organized into a kingdom under a supreme head, whose sole concern is to oppose and thwart the Kingdom of God. The origin of sin, while traced to the free choice of man, is also traced to temptation from outside sources, which, while not being either an excuse or cause for human sin, presented to man the idea of disobedience, so that it was through man's response to this temptation that he who was created immortal came under the dominion of death. The idea that there are orders of being lower than God and yet higher than man is by no means inconceivable. And it is not merely shelving the problem of evil to refer it to such a source, for it is no more inconceivable that such creatures should fall than that man should, if we are to regard sin as an abuse of freedom, and not merely something inevitable to a finite creature, or due to man's peculiar constitution and his possible inheritance from an animal ancestry. And when we look out upon the universe as a whole apart from man, it is a not absurd hypothesis that evil has intruded into a perfect scheme, for the vastness and the power and the order of the whole, down to the minutest details, display such intelligence, wisdom, might and care that it becomes all the more astonishing to find such a wonderful machine here and there, but only here and there,

THE PROBLEM OF EVIL

working to the danger or harm of mortal dwellers on this planet. The imperfection of working is so slight, so obviously not in the design of the machine or in its regular working, that it does look like a defect which cannot be traced to a mind capable of framing such a universe, and seems to be referable rather to some deliberate interference of a much smaller mind and less mighty power, but of malevolent disposition. We have not the information to enable us to construct anything like a complete picture or find a full explanation, but the idea of demonic powers is certainly in our Scriptures and cannot be dismissed as mere superstition. All down the ages there have been hints and rumours of the action of evil spirits: missioners beyond Christendom are often compelled to admit the possibility of demon possession, and modern investigation of psychic phenomena has led even sceptical observers to a similar conclusion. It is therefore not inconceivable to refer natural evils to demonic powers, and, although it is still more speculative, it is not entirely without support here and there in revelation to conceive that the animals have shared in the Fall, since we have prophecies that hostilities between animals shall one day come to an end, and also the picture in the Apocalypse of the bestial orders taking part in the worship of God. Indeed, modern observation, which is beginning to discover signs of intelligence in the animals, may still be forced to discover some degree of moral consciousness also; and if this is so, then it is not inconceivable that the animal world, as we know it to-day, has also fallen. Even evolutionary biology is compelled to assume that some of the species have chosen a line of development that has condemned them to remain on a lower level or even to suffer deterioration, and the cruelty of some of the carnivores, especially in cases where their prey is tortured or played with, may have some obscure moral cause. No one who has known much of domesticated animals would hesitate to describe them as distinguishably good or bad. To sum up, it seems possible to regard the evil in the world, when it really is evil, of whatever kind, as due to some other will than the Will of God.

The problem thus narrows itself down to whether the Creator ought to have ever offered to beings that were capable of abusing their freedom the power of doing so. And since God could not create beings of His own order, but only finite and therefore lower creatures, the problem comes down to this point, whether God ought to have created at all, because it involved not only the possibility of evil, but its foreseen actuality. To answer that question depends upon the valuation of existence which the creatures themselves hold. Now there are a great, and it is to be feared an increasing, number of people who declare that life is not worth living and existence is intolerable, since the pain outweighs the pleasure and the evil overwhelms the good. It is obvious that this verdict is not that of humanity as a whole; the people who hold it rarely follow out the logic of their belief, which would surely involve the preaching and practice of racial suicide. And it is evident that such pessimism is due to the denial of God and immortality which, whether they are true or not, cannot be denied without having precisely such results. It has been affirmed, and that with more likelihood of truth, that every creature would prefer existence to non-existence, whatever its nature.

All that we can now do is to set forth what we can deduce to be the valuation of our existence by the divine Mind, which may go far to explain why existence was planned and its possibilities permitted. Evidently God must regard freedom, even though throwing open the door to sin, and so to suffering, as better than any form of coercion. And surely, whatever some individuals may say, humanity agrees with this, else why its struggles all down history to obtain for the individual complete freedom, even though there is always the possibility that the individual may misuse it? Man's political aspirations show that here he shares the divine valuation. But we can go farther than this: the divine Mind not only permits sin but must also permit all the evil which follows it; but this not as a mere punishment, for despite what many theologians have pleaded, it is difficult to see what real satisfaction there is to the Mind of God that evil shall be consequent upon sin, if this is the end of the story. It is quite obvious that this consequence of evil upon sin has a certain redemptive promise, for there is discernible in evil a preventive purpose, in that suffering often prevents a man sinking further. Moreover, since man's nature was endowed with original righteousness and with the desire for God, sin never satisfies his soul, and between the negative dissatisfaction of sin and the positive suffering which it entails, man's spirit is at least kept alive, and in that there lies the hope of his further awakenment. Once man is awakened to his original purpose and the divine endowment, and seeks its restoration through grace, then it is found that in fighting against the evils in the world he is the more likely to progress: they bring out his strength, they compel him to recognize his dependence upon God, they invite him to a co-operation with God in the glorious task of freeing the world from all evil. Therefore sin has been permitted, because freedom is a higher state than coercion, and evil has been permitted to follow sin, because evil can act as a corrective of sin, preventing it from following its natural course which would be the death of the soul. Therefore, once man has fallen, a world like this becomes the best school and discipline for him. God did not make the evil in the world, but He does turn it to a good purpose. Moreover, all evil has the promise of being only temporary in character; it can be done away by the co-operation of man in accepting the purpose of God; the fight against evil is demanded as his reparation for sin, and is now the safest way by which man can rise; it disciplines his spirit for the gift of a perfect freedom which, because of what has happened, is now persuaded that this is to be found only in perfect surrender to the Will of God and in union with Him, and so will make any further fall impossible. The Fall has therefore been allowed in order that one possibility of freedom may be worked out, and freedom become what it is in God, freedom to do all good and freedom to do no evil.

This line of explanation seems to do more for our problem than one which would regard evil as in any way a necessity: inevitable to the deprivation which finitude entails, for infinity and perfection are not the same thing; or essential to an educative process, for God might have designed another kind of world altogether. It escapes the dilemma of regarding this world as the best of all possible worlds, which it obviously is not, for we believe in a better world to come; or, on the other hand, of attributing to God the creation of an evil world. We must admit that the world has been created imperfect; if it were not so, man would be satisfied with life here and with himself, which he is not intended to be; but imperfection does not involve evil.

THE PROBLEM OF EVIL

The existence of evil may always be a trial for faith, but it ought never to be a hindrance to faith. It is especially for Christian faith that evil becomes such a heavy problem, but it ought to be remembered that without the facts on which that faith rests, it is no problem at all. So far from the problem of evil being a hindrance to faith, apart from faith the problem is not even discernible. The discernment of evil may therefore be regarded as a sign of implicit faith; while to argue that the existence of evil is a hindrance to faith involves a position which first has to assume what it then has to deny. To reject faith is to reject the only solution, both philosophical and practical; and to allow the existence of evil to destroy faith is to condemn humanity to a paralysing pessimism in which not only hope is lost, but thought itself is condemned to futility.

IX

PRAYER AND ITS DIFFICULTIES

PRAYER is the very essence of religion, the vital breath of the saint, an exercise which can employ all the powers of the mind, become the chief occupation of life, and exercises faculties capable of exploring largely unknown areas of the spiritual realm, whose powers and possibilities are nevertheless governed by exact scientific and spiritual conditions. And yet this wonderful power remains unknown, and is left unappropriated because of its initial difficulties. Until religion expresses itself in prayer it is hardly religion at all, for religion is not only a consciousness of dependence upon a higher order of Being, but is an expression of that dependence, and the exact nature of that dependence can be set forth only in true prayer. For the dependence of the soul upon God is of a peculiar character: in one sense the dependence is absolute, for the soul depends upon God for its very existence, both for its creation and for its continuance in being; and yet the soul can live not only in ignorance and neglect of God, but even in rebellion against Him. This kind of existence is, however, so far from the intention of its Creator and so misses the end of its being, that the soul thus living, though in possession of all its faculties, is regarded as spiritually dead. It is only when the soul, con-

PRAYER AND ITS DIFFICULTIES

scious of its dependence and aware of its need, relates itself again to God by an act of will which expresses itself in an attitude of submission and aims at the attainment of perfect agreement that religion can be said to be reached, and this act of relation must begin in prayer.

The popular difficulties about prayer nearly always arise from a fundamental misunderstanding about religion. These difficulties concentrate around the petitionary element in prayer. It would be possible to evade these difficulties, which concern what is merely one element in the vast and varied activity of prayer, by excluding petitionary prayer as invalid and mistaken. Sometimes efforts are made to commend prayer to the modern mind by making it a purely subjective exercise, and attempts at substitutes are made by recommending exercises which are supposed to be equally efficacious, although they are actually deprived of all religious significance, since they amount to nothing more than concentration upon great, ennobling or helpful ideas and devices for influencing the subconscious mind by the interfusion of such ideas in order to gain health, peace or power. Even when the necessity of prayer being directed to God is recognized, it is sometimes attempted to evade the difficulties involved in God's response, by such declarations as, " He that rises from his knees a better man, his prayer is answered," or by such explanations as, " Prayer is like a rope stretched between God and ourselves ; when we pull the rope it does not bring God nearer to us, but it does bring us nearer to Him." These things may be true enough, but they avoid the difficulties only by emptying prayer of its essential characteristic and depriving it of much of its power. The fact that petition is often

PRAYER AND ITS DIFFICULTIES

wrongly regarded as the characteristic or chief element in prayer, and that it is this element which raises difficulties for many minds, must be no excuse for attempting to get rid of the difficulties by eliminating this element. Although in the higher exercise of prayer the petitionary element may shrink considerably and the difficulties connected therewith may cease to be so obtrusive, nevertheless this one element does so hold the key to the rest, that unless this is understood, the other elements of prayer, however extensively and earnestly practised, will lose their point and centre.

The difficulties of prayer are really much wider than intellectual objections; they are really threefold : *theoretical, spiritual* and *practical.*

The *theoretical difficulties* about prayer can be stated as three problems : why prayer should be necessary, how God can answer prayer, and why prayer seems so often unanswered ? It is quite obvious that on any adequate conception of God's knowledge He does not require to be informed of any of our needs, while on any worthy conception of His care for us it seems incredible that God should want to be reminded of our needs by a formal request to supply them before He will do so. But it must be remembered that for the supply of a great many of our fundamental needs no prayer is necessary : God has not only given us life without our asking for it, but He has made provision for its sustenance, both material and spiritual. The very constitution of our minds, the needs of our soul which cannot be satisfied apart from God, and the universal grace which God grants to all; the great fundamental needs, which correspond to an earthly father's provision of food and clothing and education for his children,

PRAYER AND ITS DIFFICULTIES

have all been bestowed without waiting for our prayers.

But religion is a peculiar, conscious dependence of a finite upon an infinite Person, a dependence which, however, is meant to be elevated into a relationship of communion, with the end in view of a perfect union with the will and nature of God; and it is for the passing from one stage to another that prayer becomes the natural and necessary means. There are some gifts and graces which God cannot safely bestow upon man until he is ready for them, and that readiness involves a consciousness of need, the recognition that they must come as gifts, and the attitude which humbly asks for them. It would not only be dangerous, but it would be impossible for God to endow us with the highest spiritual gifts until we were sufficiently educated, unselfish and humble to use them for right ends. The difficulties therefore vanish as soon as we make prayer sufficiently spiritual; but the difficulties seem to remain when material needs are concerned. Many of our prayers are for material things, for health, for rescue from harassing situations, for the deliverance of our friends or loved ones, and sometimes for prosperity or wealth. It would be easy to lessen the popular difficulties if it were laid down that prayer must never be for anything material, but this would be to dismiss not only the often childish and sometimes selfish prayers into which religious people have fallen, but to condemn many of the greatest saints for similar faults, and to dismiss many scriptural exhortations and promises as mistaken and misleading. It is no doubt often forgotten by those who pray that we must not ask for anything which would be bad for us or for others, or which is contrary to the all-wise and loving will of God.

PRAYER AND ITS DIFFICULTIES

The really selfish prayer is essentially irreligious, and to attempt to alter the will of God would of course be sacrilegious and, if successful, an unmitigated catastrophe. It is not, however, to be concluded that these admissions either characterize most prayer as fundamentally irreligious, or make all prayer quite useless because it cannot alter the purpose of God. There is no doubt that many of our prayers are quite foolish, and if our consideration were wider, our knowledge more educated, our wants more unselfish, and our religion deeper, we should never pray such prayers; but it is nevertheless better to pray foolishly and badly and even selfishly than not to pray at all, because the most important thing in prayer is not what we ask for, but the fact that we ask, since it implies a recognition of God's power and of our dependence upon Him. Prayer needs to be educated, but it must first be practised before that can take place; indeed, the practice of prayer is its best education, and if prayer is to begin early enough, it must often include petitions which later on we should abandon. But this does not mean that even after our wisdom and spirituality have greatly increased we should not ask God for all the things which we need, even though we may not be sure whether they are good for us, or whether God will give them to us. Prayer must proceed on the assumption that all things are possible with God, and we know that the only limit to what He will actually do lies in His goodness and wisdom. We shall therefore all through our earthly life continue to ask for things which we feel we need but which God will withhold, only we shall come to take the withholding of them as an answer to prayer as truly as if they were given. It takes very little experience of life and very little growth in sanctity to be able to look back and recognize that God never answered some of our prayers more fully than when He refused our actual request; for if He did not give what we wanted, He always gave what we really needed. But this limitation does not mean that there is no area on which prayer is free to play, and no change possible for it to bring about; for there must be a great many things which it *is* the will of God for us to have, but it is His will, and not merely an arbitrary, but a wise and loving will, that these shall be granted only when we ask for them, and perhaps only when we have asked for them passionately and persistently; for until we feel the need for them as all-important, and go on feeling it, not as a mere whim or momentary longing, but as a growing and permanent desire, it would not be wise for Him to answer us.

It is thus that the importunity of prayer is rendered necessary; such prayer, it must be understood, does not alter the will of God, but it may enable His will for us to take effect. There must be many instances where for that will to take effect in answer to our desire would demand actual alterations in material conditions or a change in the spiritual activity of God. To discuss how this may be possible brings up the question of miracle, which must be left for later discussion; but it is surely not inconceivable that God has not only left Himself freedom to alter material conditions in response to our request, if that should be good for us, but has also stored up for us spiritual power which has been reserved as accessible only to prayer. Why prayer is often unanswered ought therefore to remain no further difficulty to the mind, though it may often be a great trial to faith. It is not answered, because

PRAYER AND ITS DIFFICULTIES

it is not good that it should be, or because it is really answered in a different and superior way, as when St. Paul received additional grace instead of being relieved of his thorn in the flesh. Or the answer to prayer may be long delayed in order that our earnestness and perseverance, which are necessary to the right reception of the gift, should be thoroughly tested and proved.

These considerations should clear up the main theoretical difficulties of prayer, but it may well be suspected that these often conceal what are best called *spiritual difficulties*; for surely it is the lack of spiritual understanding that makes possible so many of the common objections, which are often childish, unconsidered, and, above all, could only arise from an extraordinary unconsciousness of our religious condition and spiritual need. It would be of little value to remove our theoretical difficulties if that did not lead to an effective exploration and a fruitful exercise of prayer; but before we can discuss practical difficulties we need to have clearly in mind the spiritual hindrances which have to be overcome. Prayer is a mental and spiritual exercise of the most exacting nature: in its essence it is the lifting up of ourselves to God, an endeavour to rise by means of communion to a perfect union with Him. It is because we have too high an opinion of our own nature, at least in its present condition, and too low an estimate of the glorious nature of God, that we are ever tempted to think that there should be no need for such an effort, or that the effort need not be great and such as to demand all our strength and employ the exercise of all our faculties. It must be remembered how our nature has suffered from the Fall; man has broken away from God, and although his

PRAYER AND ITS DIFFICULTIES

spiritual faculties may remain, they must be at least greatly weakened by neglect. It is as if muscles long disused and almost withered away were suddenly called upon to act. It is this, and not anything unnatural in prayer, that is the cause of the extraordinary inertia, and sometimes reluctance approaching almost to distaste, which are experienced when we begin the way of prayer; and not only when we begin to pray after an almost prayerless life, but often enough whenever we try to pray, the beginning is always a difficulty, while many experience a desire for prayer which seems to vanish the moment they actually begin to pray. This disinclination is sometimes so strong, and yet, if overcome, so soon passes into ease and delight in prayer, that we are almost driven to suspect some evil purpose trying to hinder us from gaining what prayer might bring; a by no means impossible hypothesis, although most often our general condition of spiritual sloth is sufficient to account for the inertia we encounter. Again, we are afflicted with spiritual insensibility; not only are our spiritual muscles stiff through lack of use, but our spiritual nerves are dull and almost paralysed, for we must be almost unconscious of our spiritual need when prayer can be so easily neglected. How different from our physical needs, which are so insistent and so easily felt! We are self-satisfied and spiritually complacent, and therefore there is so little urgency to prayer. How rarely do we hunger and thirst after righteousness, how seldom does our soul cry out for God as a thirsty land! Moreover, we are unresponsive to God's drawing; we are insensitive to His Presence all about us, which if felt would make the whole world an oratory, and we do not feel His yearning

PRAYER AND ITS DIFFICULTIES

to enter into communion with us; for our spiritual senses have not only grown dull, they are distracted by the passing of time, the dull pressure of the flesh and the allurements of the world. For we need to remember when we are discussing answers to prayer that in a sense our prayer is the answer to God's call; it is His unanswered call rather than our unanswered prayers which ought to suggest the greater difficulties to our minds. Then, again, we are spiritually ignorant, we do not know what is the will of God, at least in detail, therefore our prayers lack efficient co-operation, which prayer was designed to secure. For we have assumed that there is an area of action which God has set aside as waiting upon the co-operation of our prayer with His will, and therefore knowledge of His will must condition the perfect operation of prayer. We can always pray, "Thy will be done," but that cannot be so effective as when we know in any given circumstance and condition what His will is. But prayer itself ought to provide such an education in knowledge of His will. It is particularly in regard to intercession, whether for causes or for persons, that this knowledge is one of the conditions of prevailing prayer. We know in general that His will is our sanctification, but we do not know always what His will is for the world at any crisis, or for the welfare in any circumstances of those for whom we pray. This should not hinder intercession, for by its very exercise the spirit grows in intuition and discernment, so that the saints have often declared that they know when their prayers will be answered or when they must desist from praying for anything. But, especially when we pray for the spiritual or material welfare of our friends, for

PRAYER AND ITS DIFFICULTIES

their being kept from temptation, guided in perplexity, healed in body or released from trouble, we often feel that we cannot be sure what is best for them. But there is probably still much that we can do: we can, in thought, lift them up into the presence of God, and if we put real desire and spiritual energy into this work our intercession may bring their souls into such contact with Him that His perfect will can be done upon them. The understanding of how intercessory prayer may be effective has been greatly increased by the discovery of telepathy, and although we know very little yet how this invisible connection is established between one mind and another, or what it can actually perform, there is a tendency to explain the possible effectiveness of prayer by the operation of this purely natural law, or even to declare that intercession is nothing else than telepathy, which would reduce this gracious ministry to hypnotism at a distance. It is to be hoped, and we can be assured, that there are distinct limits to the influence that one mind can have upon another by these invisible methods, and that when our desires are first submitted to the perfect will of God and our minds seek to work upon the minds of others only through His mind, not only is there greater power obtained by this method, but that power is then rendered absolutely safe. On the other hand, it is quite possible that the discovery of the unconscious influence of mind upon mind has a great deal to teach us about the scientific understanding of prayer, though it looks as if long ago the saints knew nearly all this by their spiritual intuition and supernatural understanding. But it does help those of us who are less experienced to understand that often it may be easier for God

PRAYER AND ITS DIFFICULTIES

to work upon some rebellious or insensitive mind through a mind already consciously open to Him, and therefore in our intercession for others there should always be the offering of our whole selves to be the unseen ministers of His grace and power to others if we are fit thus to be used. Such suggestions show how intercessory prayer may avail for others when all else fails, and while we must exclude from its possibility anything like hypnotism or actual coercion of the will, there is still room for such a spiritual telepathy as will bring to the minds of some, otherwise closed, considerations, inspirations and persuasions that may make all the difference. There is no more unselfish ministry to which the soul can give itself than intercession; for the influence thus exerted, though actually divine in its origin and power, yet will have been released by our spiritual activity, which can here rise to tremendous heights; and yet the service our prayer will have rendered will never be known to anyone save God and ourselves. The possibilities this opens up explain how the withdrawal from the ordinary activities of life of those who are specially endowed and divinely called that they may give themselves to a life of prayer is by no means the selfish seclusion and useless activity which some in their ignorance have conceived it to be.

The most intractable of all the spiritual difficulties connected with prayer is spiritual sloth, which hinders the beginning and hampers the development of the prayer life. It is when we set ourselves to prayer that we discover what our spiritual condition actually is; for we find ourselves lacking in interest, in desire, and especially in the grace of perseverance. This sloth must be thrown off if we mean to live a spiritual life, and for the

PRAYER AND ITS DIFFICULTIES

effort required we must summon everything to our aid. We must consider the death of the soul to which sloth at last leads; we must face our own needs and feel the needs of others; we must remind ourselves of the all-sufficient grace of God, and of the wonderful service we can render; and we should inflame our minds with spiritual ambition by studying the science of prayer and remembering the reward that its exercise brought to the great saints. It is possible to fall into the temptation of reading a great deal about prayer instead of giving ourselves to its practice, and there is a subtle danger in reading treatises on advanced mystical experience, because they may lead us into thinking that we are farther on than we really are, because of the faint reproduction in our own souls which mystical language induces. But the very fact that it is often of such profound interest to read works on prayer, and that we can feel a stirring in our souls when we are reading of the mystical experiences of others, should rather be an encouragement to the deliberate and consistent practice of prayer. It is encouraging to know that men of like passions as ourselves have found their way into the ultimate secrets of this wonderful exercise, and it is stimulating to know that there are vast areas mapped out far in advance of those we have yet reached, so that we need never lose our way; indeed, there are whole continents yet to be explored, so that we need never fear that our prayer life shall lack variety, adventure, or the possibility of still further progress.

Directions for the actual practice of prayer must be looked for elsewhere in treatises devoted to the subject and written by those who are acknowledged masters; but something may be said concerning the *practical difficulties* of prayer, at least of the

PRAYER AND ITS DIFFICULTIES

more elementary kind. The most common of these are the lack of time, the invasion of distractions, and the dullness and distaste which are often due to disorder and lack of variety in our prayers. So many complain that they have no *time* for prayer. Theoretically time is not necessary; in itself the pure activity of the soul is as free from time as it is from space: a moment's swift desire, if sincere and wholehearted, will accomplish more than mere length of time and ceaseless repetition. And this is how it is that we can be exhorted to " pray without ceasing," which is to have the desire of the soul permanently directed towards God, although the conscious expression of this desire must necessarily be intermittent. But practically time is necessary. If we are to get into the true attitude and right condition for prayer, we need a quiet and concentrated mind, and this often takes some time to secure; and if we are to reach down to the depths of the spirit and discover what its desires really are, we may have to work through all kinds of superficial concerns, while it may take time to stir the sluggish soul to action, and still more to set it on fire with love and longing. This is why the common objection to fixed times of prayer, on the plea that one only ought to pray when one feels like it, is so foolish: we can never know whether we feel like prayer until we have been trying to pray for some time. Moreover, if our soul is not in time, our minds and our bodies certainly are; and if we are going to influence our whole nature, then we must literally soak ourselves in prayer, we must hold the spirit still before God, we must "wait upon the Lord." It is interesting to notice that in the higher stages of prayer, the timeless nature of the soul makes itself known by the obliteration of all sense of passing time; so that while it is true that a momentary, intense desire may lift the soul to God, it is also true that such a desire may hold the soul in that one activity while time slips by unnoticed. But the busiest of us can make room for more time; if we would only seize those periods when the soul is freshest or is in greatest need, only a little more time set apart for regular prayer might make a very great difference. What those who complain of lack of time really mean is lack of desire, for desire would make time. What must be done can be done. But in general it might be advised that everyone might rise a little earlier and thus steal a few minutes from sleep to make room for prayer, though it is advisable not to make the time immediately before going to bed a main time for prayer, as one is then often too tired; earlier in the evening is a far better time. But during the most crowded day change of work, or the striking of the clock, may be used as occasions for a moment's recollection; churches can be visited where solitude is difficult to obtain at home; and walks in lonely or even in crowded places may be profitably used for prayer. If desire is really strong, we have got rid of the idea that we are wasting time in prayer, and when we have come to find it a delight to commune with God, this problem of time will solve itself even for the busiest persons and most overcrowded lives.

Distractions present a more persistent and intractable difficulty. They are probably intensified by our modern habits of life which, with its lack of leisure and over-stimulation, leaves our minds so restless that concentration has become almost impossible to us. When we get alone and quiet for prayer, worries, duties and trifling con-

PRAYER AND ITS DIFFICULTIES

cerns crowd the more into mind. This is psychologically quite explicable, for these things have been pushed aside when we have been engaged with other occupations and now seize the opportunity to get themselves attended to. We must not make the invasion of distractions into a further distraction by letting their disturbance worry and harass our souls. We need to remember that it is the depth and sincerity of desire, and not the accurate expression of it or the time spent, that counts with God; though the absence of distraction and the time that can be spent in holding the soul in conscious desire undoubtedly increase the subjective efficacy of prayer. But we must be careful not to lose patience with ourselves; the mind must be steadily herded back again from its wandering and excursions, and these efforts will in time have the desired effect. It is a useful thing to make a break of complete silence before attempting to pray, perhaps even to sit down for a little and let distractions have their way with us until the mind has disposed of them; some physical action like counted breathing, or such forms of prayer as the recitation of the Rosary, or saying carefully and aloud some of the great prayers of the saints, may be found a help towards gaining concentration, achieving quiet of mind and awakening desire. The best protection against distraction is the use of ordered, which means pre-ordered prayer. It is well to know before we begin what we intend to pray for and to have in mind some simple divisions. But a great deal of distraction and even dryness in prayer is due to the vast range of its exercise being imperfectly known and only one or other of its main elements being used. The main elements of prayer may be classified under seven heads, and

PRAYER AND ITS DIFFICULTIES

if prayer is to be kept balanced, varied, and full it ought to include them all: adoration, confession, meditation, petition, intercession, and dedication. These need not be necessarily all used at any period of prayer, nor need they all occupy the same amount of time, but within the course of one's daily prayers some place should be secured for each. It is because these different elements are reduced in popular understanding and practice to petition alone that intellectual difficulties about prayer have loomed so large, while prayer has seemed so uninteresting and vain to those who have made only slight and uninstructed experiments. Prayer must necessarily embrace all these elements if it is to be true prayer, because they are essential stages in the lifting up of the soul to God, and petition has no right place save in this setting. If a simple rule is made for securing sufficient times of prayer, however short, during the day, and a place be given to these varying elements, the prayer-life becomes of extraordinary interest, quite apart from its necessity as the acknowledgment we owe to God, or the health and efficiency it imparts to the soul. And if only it were known what certainty in God, and delight in Him, what spiritual peace and power are to be attained by the steady, sincere and scientific practice of prayer, difficulties would keep no one back, for it is in this exercise that the soul at last begins to live its true life of conscious communion, to be consummated in its true end, union with God.

X

MIRACLES

MIRACLES were once counted among the greatest aids to faith; they were evidence of the divine commission to a prophet; they have been regarded as necessary for the canonization of a saint; but they have now long been felt to be rather a hindrance to belief and a difficulty for faith. The mere fact that the Bible contains a record of miracles is for many sufficient to discredit its testimony on any point whatsoever, for it has come to be almost a dogma of modern thought that miracles cannot happen. This change of view is due, first of all, to the scientific conception that the universe is bound together by an unalterable sequence of physical cause and effect, and that any interference with these is inconceivable. It is the prevalence of this idea that has led to the fixed conclusion that such a thing as a miracle cannot happen.

It might be thought that the whole question was simply whether miracles happen or not, and that this might be easy to determine. But there are, firstly, difficulties about the value of evidence, and this eventually will be influenced by the conviction whether or not miracles can happen. Secondly, whether any event is a miracle depends upon the definition of a miracle. Therefore both these questions must be discussed before we can fairly decide the simple issue.

It might well be that a miracle is only an interference with the course of nature, like that which is undoubtedly wrought by man. Man does interfere with the natural course of things, if never by changing the normal behaviour of any physical element, yet by bringing about a new combination; and this human activity introduced into the natural sequence has certainly accomplished what nature would never have done left to itself, and indeed altered the appearance of nature, and yet without what could be called a breach of natural law. It is only by learning how nature acts and utilizing that knowledge that man is able to produce new action. Therefore, it would seem to be no contradiction of the general order prevailing in nature to believe that God is capable of exercising even greater changes through the perfect knowledge which He as Creator of nature must possess, and through His more immediate and omnipresent contact with it. Therefore, it has generally been admitted, even by sceptical thinkers, that if God exists miracles would not be incredible.

But even when the existence of God is accepted, a still further objection against miracles is urged from the basis of a semi-religious or philosophical conception of God. It is argued that for God to need to work a miracle is a reflection upon His wisdom and foresight; it looks like a necessity for altering or rectifying His work, which only a poor workman, or one who had forgotten something, would ever need to do. If nature is the creation of God, it ought not to need alteration or interference. This argument has a stronger appeal, for it will not do to say that miracles are an essential expression of the freedom of God, for when the physical universe was created, that freedom could surely have been used in such a way as to make any alteration unnecessary. But that same freedom could also have been used to leave room for miracles. The real answer to the difficulty, therefore, must be sought in deeper considerations. We have seen that the creation of the physical universe was neither a necessity to God nor to supply any need of His, but was for the purpose of training finite souls to share in the Divine nature. Now it is part of the constitution of man as an incarnate being that he shall come under the dominion of two spheres, the physical and the spiritual, and therefore for God to establish perfect relations with men, to reveal Himself to them in a convincing way, there will need to be action in both realms, so that beside the knowledge of God obtained through considering the physical world, there is obviously room, and there may be need, for God to manifest Himself not only indirectly through the frame of the physical world, and directly upon the spirit of men, but also by distinct direct action of His Spirit upon the physical world. Moreover, it has to be considered that by the Fall man has established wrong relations with the physical order, and dimmed the clear knowledge he might have obtained from that order, so that other than purely natural or purely spiritual means may be necessary for God to reveal Himself to man and rescue him from some of the natural consequences of his sin. This immediate activity of God upon nature is therefore something which is specially necessary in view of the purpose of Creation, in view of man's constitution, and in view of his special spiritual need since he has come

MIRACLES

under the reign of sin. The physical world cannot perfectly manifest the nature of God; it was created for a specific purpose. Man does not wholly belong to this realm, but was placed here in order to be educated for another; therefore, at least for man's sake, room must be left for the higher activity known as miracle. This need involve the breach of no law, natural or spiritual, but only a new combination of both, and it certainly involves no lack of foresight on the part of God, for an area for this freedom had to be left if the needs of man were to be fully met.

But there is a third objection to miracles based upon the uncertainty of human veracity, which makes all evidence for anything extraordinary open to question, because of the possibility of misunderstanding and the untrustworthiness of human testimony. To this objection the fullest consideration must be given. Human testimony to a miracle is likely to err in three directions: it can be, firstly, a deliberate invention; man's very relation to the spiritual world makes him discontented with the ordinary happenings of life and the unbroken habit of nature; he craves something more wonderful, he desires wider possibilities, he loves the element of surprise. This craving sometimes leads him to tell lies; we have therefore to be sure that the witnesses to any miracle were unlikely to be tempted or to yield in this particular direction. If a man is going to benefit greatly by telling a story of a miracle we may well have suspicions; whereas if he is likely to be put to death because he tells such a story there is less chance that it will be a piece of pure invention on his part. But, secondly, even if there is no sheer invention, there can often be exaggeration; this

MIRACLES

can make something which originally was not very remarkable appear quite wonderful. Whenever a man tells a story of any happening that was out of the way it rarely loses anything in the telling; the vastness, the surprise, the effects are all often exaggerated. But although this factor may come into play more often, yet it is not likely that imagination will often start off with something perfectly normal; its tendency is to exaggerate, but there will always be something which, because of its unusual character, prompts exaggeration. Therefore, if many stories of quite incredible miracles are told about certain persons we might doubt them, but we might believe that that person was somewhat extraordinary, and possibly did some things out of the normal. Here the test will be for the consistency of the alleged miracles with the general character of the person. Thirdly, human evidence is sometimes based on a misunderstanding; a thing may be regarded as a miracle merely because it is not understood how it is done; it may be by a perfectly natural law, and therefore not be a miracle at all. It is not only sound, but necessary, that all these tests should be applied to the evidence for miracles, for although Hume's famous dilemma, that no amount of human testimony would be sufficient to establish a miracle, obviously makes an impossible and unscientific demand, yet it has this value, that a miracle does demand testimony from witnesses who can be trusted, that there must be evidence that it is not due to imagination, and that it cannot be explained as the operation of some natural law of which the witnesses are simply ignorant.

Although modern thought, until recently, has been almost closed against the possibility of miracles, yet to-day the resistance against accepting the evidence for them is not nearly so strong as once it was. It is acknowledged by most people who think deeply enough that everything is ultimately miraculous, that is to say, it is not really explained by cause and effect. Hume long ago showed that there is no more reason for believing in cause and effect than that we constantly see one thing happening after another; the cause does not explain the effect. Nor does it follow that when things happen constantly they are thereby explained; that they always do happen so is, in a sense, still more remarkable. Again, the element of miracle is not eliminated by the insertion of a long process of minute changes; why one thing should ever become another is from the point of view of the human mind a miracle; it can only understand things always remaining the same. The insertion of a vast number of small changes in between one thing and another, so far from explaining it, simply increases the number of miracles. With this outlook all existence is a miracle, for there seems no necessity for anything existing at all; and how the existent ever arose from the non-existent must always remain a stupendous miracle. To this attitude the existence of a few more miracles makes no difference; and yet it does not meet the difficulty about miracles. Physical cause and physical effect may not be self-explained, existence may not be self-explained; but what is meant by miracle is an unusual effect, or one which no usual cause could produce, and however miraculous the whole world may be, that would be an unusual miracle. The attitude of modern science is certainly less dogmatic in excluding miracles than it once was; it has recognized that what we call the laws

MIRACLES

of nature are only generalizations and averages which have to embrace many exceptions and divergences. It is believed, too, that there are many forces and powers in the universe which science has not discovered, and which can never be scientifically explained. Moreover, the idea that the universe is a self-contained physical system is being scientifically questioned. It looks much more likely that it rests upon an invisible reservoir of force from which it is being constantly replenished. But even this attitude would only sanction the idea that what are now called miracles are simply the action of other laws at present unknown, that is, they will cease to be called miracles when our knowledge is sufficiently extended. There is no doubt that a great difference in the attitude of the modern mind has been made by psychical research. Although many of the phenomena alleged to take place are still under dispute, and differently constituted minds trace them to different causes, the possibility of the immediate action of spirit upon matter outside the normal channels of contact is of sufficient weight to inhibit dogmatic denial. Moreover, it does look as if the powers which create these phenomena are not entirely reducible to natural law; they are powers which only certain types of personality possess.

The discovery of the far-reaching influence of suggestion has prompted the theory that the numerous healing miracles claimed to have been wrought by Christ were instances of the use of this power, and therefore the stories of this kind contained in the New Testament are widely admitted, because they are thought to have been made more credible. But neither is this attitude sufficient to establish that miracles have happened.

MIRACLES

It is very doubtful whether many of Christ's miracles can come under the head of healing by suggestion, and all of them certainly cannot. Not only the immediacy of some of the cures recorded, but the nature of them still surpasses anything that modern mental therapeutics can accomplish. These considerations have only created a new atmosphere and enabled us to approach the subject with fewer presuppositions; they are by no means proof that miracles take place. Indeed, the movement of the modern argument seems to be somewhat in this direction: it is no longer dogmatically denied that miracles are possible; it is admitted by many that there seems sufficient evidence that some stories of miracles are true; but the conclusion is that they were not really miracles. We have therefore moved swiftly from the older idea that miracles are impossible, to the conclusion that anybody could work a miracle if he only knew how. It is obvious that this does not establish what religion means by miracles. This unexpected conclusion is probably due to the fact that there is confusion as to what actually constitutes a miracle.

The word miracle only means a happening that causes wonder, but its specific use by religion means something more than that. It means that it is something really wonderful, the wonder of which cannot be explained away, because it is to be traced to the direct action of God, even though it may be wrought through some human agent. It is not therefore a miracle unless it has some physical effect. This therefore excludes striking conversions, or heroic virtue produced by grace; it does not include what is sometimes called "the miracle of the Altar," namely, the change in the

MIRACLES

elements of bread and wine by which they are believed to become the Body and Blood of Christ, for the change is not physically visible. The working of some wonderful effect by occult power would not be called a miracle; which would therefore exclude the things alleged to have been done by the Egyptians in imitation of the miracles wrought by Moses, as it would also exclude the casting-out of demons which Jesus acknowledged the sons of the Pharisees could perform. Therefore, even if modern mental therapeutics could do all the works which were done by Jesus, they would not be reckoned as miracles, for it is believed that whatever knowledge and use of mental therapeutics Jesus employed, His wonderful works were really due to the direct action of God. In regarding any work as a miracle because it must be ascribed to the direct action of God, there is involved not only the question of a power employed, such as ordinary nature does not reveal, but that power must be employed consistently with the character of God. Miracles must therefore have a religious purpose.

The names used to describe miracles in the New Testament bring out the essential characteristics of a miracle: they are called by three Greek words which can be translated, *wonders, powers, signs*. *Wonders* draws attention to the effect they create in the minds of the observers; *powers* indicates that they are not due to natural means; and *signs* implies that they were wrought as a means of revelation. From these New Testament terms we may proceed to notice the scholastic definition of a miracle. This employs a threefold classification; namely, a miracle may be a manifestation of power *above, outside* or *contrary* to the natural order. A miracle is regarded as *above* the natural order if

MIRACLES

it simply accomplishes what nature never could accomplish, such as the bringing of a dead person to life. It is said to be *outside* the natural order if it has an effect which natural powers might conceivably produce, but never do, for these powers are here extended beyond their ordinary operation; for instance, a man might have his withered hand cured by a long natural process, but if it is quite suddenly healed, then this is something outside the natural order. A miracle is said to be *contrary* to nature when what is wrought seems in defiance of natural powers, namely, in such an act as that of walking on the water. Now it is the last class of miracle, described as contrary to nature, which it is difficult for the modern mind to accept as possible. We must, however, be careful that the scholastic definition is rightly understood. *Contrary to nature* does not mean that which is a violation of the law of nature; Augustine is often quoted when he speaks of miracle as something that is contrary to nature *as it is known;* but such a definition does not bring out the essential characteristic of miracles, for it would imply that if only we knew the laws or forces at present obscured from us, we should know that the thing was not a miracle at all. The issue is better set forth in the analogy we have previously considered, namely, that of the interference of human personality in the material world; a man never breaks nature's laws, but he often uses one to correct the operation of another. For instance, gravitation is a name for the fact that masses are drawn to one another in proportion to their mass and in inverse ratio to their distance. We can not only prevent this happening, or even reverse it, as when a man catches a cricket ball and throws it back again, but we can actually use the tendency

MIRACLES

to gravitate to reverse the process, as for instance in a lift which is worked by balancing weights. In the same way we may believe that God changes the order of nature, not by a real infraction of that order, but by the direct action of His own mind, which, since it is also the author of the natural order, cannot be said in any way to infringe it. No doubt, also, all such actions of God are governed by law in the sense that they are governed by His consistency; but we may not always know what is consistent to the mind of God.

The whole issue is now narrowed down to this: that miracles are possible, they are consistent with the purpose of God, and so whether they happen or not is entirely a matter of evidence. Now, as we have already seen, evidence is a very difficult thing to make absolutely certain, and this is not wholly due to the fact that so much of it lies in the past or is second-hand. Current events of an extraordinary character are continually being reported, but whether or not they actually happen it is extraordinarily difficult to decide. It is possible to read a book concerning psychical phenomena in which the phenomena are testified to by scientific men, and fraud is carefully eliminated, and yet to be left in complete doubt as to whether these things really happened or not. Twenty witnesses of trained capacity may be present at the same manifestation but very rarely will the twenty agree as to whether anything happened, or as to whether there was anything supernormal about it. Striking things which have happened to one often seem less striking when looked back upon, and unless an account was immediately written down they may come to be doubted. Again, it is felt by many religious people that the reported evidence for miracles is of differing value. Some would be inclined to accept stories of miracles found in the Bible more readily than they would accept the miracles traditionally ascribed to the saints; they might be still more doubtful about miracles said to be wrought by non-religious people; while about the stories of miracles contained in pagan authors of antiquity they would be entirely unbelieving. The distinction may be quite unsound: the evidence for some of the ecclesiastical miracles, as they are called, for instance, of some of the cures wrought at the shrine of St. Thomas à Becket, is almost overwhelming, while it is almost impossible to doubt the stories of some of the remarkable cures which have taken place at Lourdes; moreover, we have no reason to reject the idea that God might use miraculous manifestations to speak to pagan peoples, or to persuade men of modern times. But the distinction, although due to prejudice, may be defended on the ground that the general character, purpose and setting of miraculous occurrences is on a higher level in the biblical narrative than elsewhere, and therefore accords better with the definition of a miracle as a Divine sign, and so is more credible.

It will be felt, however, by some that even the biblical miracles stand on different levels; though the reason the biblical miracles have superior credence given them is because they fit in with the general purpose of Revelation, to which the Bible is a unique witness. It has been noted that miracles are not scattered either haphazard or regularly throughout the biblical narrative, but they group themselves round certain periods, namely: the Deliverance of Israel from captivity and the establishment of the Theocracy; the inauguration of the Prophetic Ministry; the Incarnation and

MIRACLES

the establishment of the Church. There are long periods of history in which no miracle is recorded to have taken place: Elijah and Elisha work miracles, but none is recorded of Amos or Jeremiah; Jesus is the greatest worker of miracles in the Bible, but no miracle is recorded of His contemporary John the Baptist. Therefore the general occurrence of miracles in the Bible does give ground for thinking that there is a consistent purpose behind them and this makes the evidence more acceptable.

We cannot here discuss the relative credibility of the different strata of biblical miracles, still less individual miracles; but it is round the miracles ascribed to Jesus Christ that the issue becomes important and capable of decision. We might glance at some of the attempts that have been made to explain away the stories of Christ's miracles. It has been suggested that they are legendary growths arising originally from quite ordinary circumstances. But although we might here and there detect a slight increase in the wonder of certain of His works as they are told by subsequent Evangelists, it would be impossible to reduce whatever exaggeration there may be to zero as their starting-point. When all allowances for growth have been made, Christ must still have been a doer of many mighty works. To remove miracle from the Gospels would leave very little behind, and that untrustworthy. For a long time it was attempted to explain the miracles as misunderstandings of some happy coincidence, as, for instance, the feeding of the multitude is explained as due to everyone producing what they had and by being satisfied with very little; similarly, the storm happened to cease at the moment Jesus commanded it; but this constant coincidence would become in

MIRACLES

itself a miracle. Such explanations bear no resemblance whatever to the Gospel story, and would involve not only the narrators, but Christ Himself, in the most childish deception. We have seen also that the stories of many of Christ's cures are admitted as genuine, because the discoveries of mental therapeutics have made it possible to look at the evidence in a quite different light. But the admission of some cures carries us by inevitable stages to the admission of practically all; for if we admit those cures wrought by Christ of which we have sufficient parallel in modern examples to believe them possible, there is no canon of literary criticism which enables us to believe that in these instances the Evangelist has told us the truth, and at the same time to reject everything that is not made credible by modern evidence. Once all were rejected; now some are admitted; it is only another step to admit all. Or take another case: suppose it was thought that the evidence concerning the raising of Jairus' daughter did not mean that she was really dead, but only in a trance; if it were so explained, then many would accept it as an historical fact, although they might have to admit that it still involved a very wonderful and sudden cure. But if the Evangelists were right in telling this story, it is no sound criticism to argue that they must be wrong when they tell the story of the raising of the widow of Nain's son, or of Lazarus, just because it is obvious that here we are dealing with people really dead. If we take the actual recorded words of Christ and the support they give to narrative, and the fact that His miracles were the wrought because of His compassion for suffering and as a sign of the Divine attitude towards it, in conjunction with the admission that a great many of the stories are credible, and yet that they go beyond anything paralleled in modern cures, then we seem to possess very strong evidence that miracles have actually happened.

The evidence for one miracle or a whole series of miracles does not establish any or every story of miraculous happening; every miracle must be tested by the general conditions of satisfactory evidence. And miracles as a whole should perhaps not be made to bear the weight once placed upon them; belief in their occurrence is no decisive test of faith; but the general admission of their possibility and the evidence for their actual occurrence is an important point to have gained. All that now needs to be recognized is the place that miracle holds in the economy of God. Miracle corresponds to the freedom possessed by the human mind in its contact with nature, but with this difference—that there is no theoretical limit to the possibility of what God can do; the only actual limit is in His wisdom and consistency. The value of belief in miracle is, first of all, that it saves us from the wholesale rejection of the story of Revelation; secondly, it keeps the human mind always open to higher possibilities, taking us beyond mechanical rigidity and illegitimate limitations; but thirdly, it makes us constantly dependent upon God; for according to the true definition of a miracle we can never ourselves expect to work miracles merely by the acquirement of greater knowledge or even greater saintliness, nor can we be certain that God will ever work a miracle in any given circumstance, however great we ourselves may think the need to be. All things are possible with God, but all things are not expedient for us; and thus while the belief in miracle opens the mind to the continual possibility of the

MIRACLES

direct intervention of God, it yet never allows us to calculate, dictate or presume. The belief in miracle is, therefore, an essential element in a truly religious interpretation of God's relations to man and the world.

XI

THE INSTINCT FOR RELIGION

THE question whether religion is instinctive to man is very difficult to decide, because of the popular confusion existing as to what is meant by "instinct," and because of the difficulty of finding a sufficiently scientific definition of religion. And yet it is a question that we are bound to ask if we want to know whether religion is fundamental to man and a universal necessity to our race. It would raise less difficult questions if we were content to speak of the religious consciousness, or even of the religious temperament; for religion is certainly a need of which many persons are acutely aware. On the other hand, there are many persons, and amongst civilized peoples they are now perhaps approximating to a majority, who have no such consciousness of either the reality or the need of religion. When, therefore, religion remains so passionate a necessity for some, and others have declared they feel no need for it whatsoever, it is natural to think that it must be a matter of temperament, like that of the artist or the musician. If a person has an impulse to express himself in artistic work, or has a passionate love for music, it is acknowledged that this can become not only a dominant concern, but, at least for that person's mental happiness, a positive necessity. But it is equally true that others seem almost without any such desire, and this creates so complete a divergence that the two types are hardly

THE INSTINCT FOR RELIGION

able to understand one another; a person with artistic sensibility feeling pity or almost contempt for those who have no such thing, and the person without it being perplexed or even amused at what seems to be the inexplicable infatuation of the artistic temperament. Is religion something of the same order: merely a matter of temperament? The complete divergence of the religious from the non-religious type, and the great difficulty of the one understanding the other, seem to support this idea; and if it is true, we can only settle down to an attempt at mutual toleration. But this is the one thing that the religious person will not do; not so much because the religious person is naturally intolerant or aggressive, he is often nothing of the kind; but the acceptance of such a position would cast doubt upon the reality and truth of religion. The phenomenon of one single person for whom religion had no sort of necessity would create the intolerable dilemma, either that God did not exist, or that the non-religious person was not truly human. Religion is so very much more important than a craving for artistic expression or musical enjoyment that it is impossible to refer it to individual temperament.

If then we are compelled to assume that religion is a natural necessity to man, should it not be classified as a human instinct? Yet there are few psychologists who would include religion amongst the instincts of man; and few theologians would demand it, mainly because it would be admitted by them that religion rarely functioned in man in such a way as to be properly described as instinctive. For the term instinct, although often used in a loose sense, as when we speak of a man having an instinct for beauty or truth, is generally limited, for the purposes of scientific discrimination, to

THE INSTINCT FOR RELIGION

describe an innate tendency common to a whole species, and in particular, is used to describe certain habits common to creatures, as for instance, the habit of some animals to store up food for the winter; of birds to build nests in which to lay their eggs and bring up their brood; of certain species of insects who deposit their eggs in the bodies of living creatures upon which the larvæ can afterwards feed. These habits are called instincts, because they are actions which seem to indicate foresight and provision demanding a very high order of intelligence, which nevertheless it seems impossible to ascribe to animals, birds or insects. The existence of such instincts is not only an interesting phenomenon, but creates a curious problem; for instincts apparently take the place among the lower creation of intelligence in man, and wherever it is necessary to assume intelligence, there we find instincts becoming fewer and less certain. We seem compelled to assume that a superior intelligence has implanted these instincts; although it has been widely assumed in scientific circles that instinct has developed by natural selection. But this is extremely difficult to accept, because of the complicated action that some instincts demand; for, by hypothesis, they would have to evolve very slowly, and yet they would be quite valueless to the species until they were perfect. We have evidence of such evolution, and therefore it seems necessary to look to intelligent guidance rather than to natural selection as the cause of evolution. On the other hand, the theologian would hesitate to ascribe instinct simply and directly to the impress of the intelligence of the Creator upon unintelligent being, because in many cases it involves what looks like cruelty, which a beneficent intelligence might surely have evaded by adopting some other way.

THE INSTINCT FOR RELIGION

Modern psychology relieves the difficulty by assuming that mind can exist and can carry out intelligent processes without being conscious, and therefore that consciousness is a development by which individual intelligence comes to replace racial instinct. This conception of an unconscious mind raises, however, enormous difficulties. An unconscious mind is almost a contradiction in terms; especially if we cannot refer it to the creation of pre-existing Conscious Mind; for then also there would seem no need for the emergence of consciousness, since instinct is often equal, if sometimes not superior to, conscious intelligence; especially if it is evolved only to be finally eclipsed. It looks rather as if consciousness had been evolved for ethical reasons, and therefore must be traced to the guidance of a pre-existing ethical consciousness, namely, to God. But these are questions psychology refuses to consider, as beyond its province, but so long as it does so, and yet concludes that consciousness is a natural evolution from unconscious mind, it must always appear as not only superficial and evasive, but such a conclusion must be regarded as highly unsatisfactory and hardly likely to be true.

Nevertheless, it remains an interesting question for psychology and one highly important to answer, even if we are to find an ultimate solution only in a deeper realm, namely, whether religion can be regarded as an instinct, and if so, whether it will be replaced by something else as man becomes more conscious. The difficulty of regarding religion as an instinct is that by an instinct is meant an animal habit; and even if man shares some instincts with the animals, religion is not animal, but is distinctive of man. The term instinct has, nevertheless, been used of religion because it is so universal among the human species, and there is no

THE INSTINCT FOR RELIGION

reason why man should not have instincts peculiar to himself. Moreover, some psychologists have tried to trace religion to an instinct. We must therefore examine the matter by enquiring what instincts man actually does possess, whether religion is one of them, or can be reduced to one of them, or whether it is merely something transitional between instinct and consciousness. Psychologists are not agreed as to how many instincts man possesses, but they would mostly agree that man has at least three, and these are: food, sex and fear; and many would agree to the addition of a fourth, namely, acquisitiveness. For these are found also among the animals, and they are cravings which are almost irresistible in man. But the moment we agree to these four, a distinction in their strength is noticeable. Fear, sex and acquisitiveness can be almost entirely overcome by man, at least as far as their expression in act is concerned, though the feeling or craving may remain; whereas the craving for food must be satisfied if man is to live, but even this craving could be defied by a man bent on suicide by starvation. And when this distinction is made, it will be further noticed that man's instincts are so unlike those of the animals that it is very doubtful whether they can be called instincts at all. Acquisitiveness, which is one of the strongest of human instincts, so that even a baby wants to clutch almost everything it sees, is not found nearly so strongly in the animals; and although a baby craves food, and will cry for it, it cannot do without exterior guidance as to where food can be obtained, or what would be good for it; it will suck by mere reaction, but unfortunately almost anything put in its mouth, whereas the newly-hatched chicken will almost immediately pick up its natural food. It is very doubtful

THE INSTINCT FOR RELIGION

whether even sex is quite instinctive to man; for we have no means of discovering whether man would even know how to satisfy his sexual cravings apart from communicated knowledge. Whatever instinct is, it is something very different in man from what it is in the lower creation. If then we are willing to give to such things as food, sex, fear, acquisitiveness, the name of instinct, cannot we regard religion also as an instinct, in the sense that this term carries when applied to human beings?

We are inclined to give to religion this instinctive value, because it is so widespread a phenomenon of the human race. Religion is almost as difficult to define as instinct, but some such definition as " the feeling of a need for coming into relationship with higher powers " would be generally accepted as wide enough to embrace all the phenomena recognized as religious. But the difficulty of getting a good working definition of religion is due not only to the widely differing phenomena that must be embraced under the term, and to the fact that much religion then seems to be unconscious of its object, but to the suggestion having been made that the whole phenomenon of religion is traceable to one or other of the fundamental instincts of man working under a disguise. This is held, firstly, because it is believed that religion can always be analysed into something more simple and fundamental, and secondly, because as man attains higher consciousness religion tends to disappear. We shall examine this second suggestion first.

It must certainly be admitted that it is in primitive communities that we find religious customs most universally observed. We shall have to postpone any full account of religious customs and the conclusions to be drawn from them until we come to deal with Comparative Religion. But here it may

THE INSTINCT FOR RELIGION

be stated that in primitive communities religion seems to express itself almost wholly in ceremonies, that often no reason can be given for their performance, and that only at a later stage of development has there to be given an explanation of why they should be performed, if their continuance is to be maintained. As a result of this questioning and of the inadequacy of the explanation given the ceremonial expression of religion comes to be dropped, because it is believed either that their object can be attained in another way, or that the whole object is mistaken. With the dropping of the universal observance of ceremonies, we are left with a religion that exists specifically and almost wholly as an interior attitude, and for a great many people therefore ceases to exist at all. It does therefore seem as if religion was once instinctive and is now ceasing to be so; and as this instinct is summoned to give an account of itself before consciousness, it is likely to be discredited and is often threatened with disappearance. But a temporary diminution in between an instinctive and a conscious religion is precisely what we might expect from similar processes in other developments, and evidence is not wanting that, despite the undisputed decline in public worship and in private religious belief, modern man is showing symptoms that he will not be able to do without religion much longer. Without a common religion it is found increasingly impossible to live a common life; the increase of the economic struggle, the self-devouring habits of industrialism, the menace of internationl war, and the possibilities of racial sterility are compelling all thinking men to face the fundamental basis of life afresh, and the pressure of these forces upon even the thoughtless is preventing anyone from remaining unconcerned. And yet there seems little likelihood of discovering any agree-

THE INSTINCT FOR RELIGION

ment which will solve our economic and international strifes unless all men can come to recognize a higher end in life than the merely economic or secular, and can be made responsive to the appeal for a loyalty to something higher than country or even humanity itself. Moreover, the sense of personal misery is mounting ever higher amongst civilized and educated people, as life lived without religion manifests its utter lack of guidance, purpose and hope; for materialistic science holds out no final hope for humanity, intellectual speculations without faith end in contradictions and uncertainty, and life confined to earth has no meaning. The personal interior life of humanity shows dangerous signs of dissolving in anarchy as religious faith comes to be given up and the moral restraints it has taught are abandoned. Strange, vague fears invade the consciousness of man, and at length threaten him with paralysing panic. Personality develops what are known as "complexes," in which dissociated centres of feeling and thought set up what seems like a life of their own, defy all rational control, and yet manifest their unhealthy nature in nervous habits, in a dangerous diminution of vitality believed to be due to their repressed conflicts, and may even threaten the mind with what is called double personality, or with the more radical disorders of insanity. It has been through the endeavour to relieve minds so affected of their intolerable condition that modern psychology has been compelled to consider afresh the fact of religion.

It has been discovered by modern clinical psychology how profoundly religion enters into the mental structure of mankind. By the very limitation of its subject psychology does not concern itself with the question whether there is any objective reality answering to religion, and this limitation compels

THE INSTINCT FOR RELIGION

psychology to a certain superficiality of concern and enquiry; while at the same time its legitimate practical limitation for the purpose of its work may induce the belief that it does not matter whether religion has an objective reality, and often produces suspicion that it has not. These are illegitimate deductions from the limitations of psychology and must not be allowed to pass without challenge; but psychology has at least done this service to religion: it has discovered its persisting power within the area of man's mind, and that it is often operative when a man thinks he is entirely beyond its influence. In some cases religion may form a complex in the mind, which a man is unwilling to submit to rational enquiry, or which he keeps separate from all his other concerns, as it were, in a water-tight compartment; but the apparent absence of religious concern is often due to the fact that it has been repressed, while a violent anti-religious attitude is often due to a conflict with irrepressible religious elements within. The ideal of modern therapeutic psychology is to secure harmony within the actual area of a man's own mind by securing a balance between his various cravings, and by bringing his complexes up into consciousness; therefore, it is disposed to demand only that place for religion, and that attitude towards it which will help to produce this result. But we have yet to be assured that this method of securing the harmony of the existing elements of the mind is going to be a lasting cure for man's mental and affectional disorders; and until it has been established that this is all that needs to be done, we need not pay too much attention to the idea that religion is merely a constitutive element of the human mind, and need not be referred to anything outside or above the mind; while we welcome the discovery that religion is at least such a strong feeling that it cannot be disregarded, and any attempt to put it out of mind altogether is bound to result in dangerous disorder. In these circumstances the verdict of a merely clinical psychology, interested chiefly in pathological cases, as to the universal value and objective validity of religion need not carry much weight, especially as different schools of psychological therapeutics differ greatly on this issue.

We can, however, examine the various psychological estimates of religion, and see whether any of them postulates an adequate cause, or offers any consistent explanation even on purely psychological principles. In the main we find that religion is conceived to be one of three things: it is an unhealthy complex, a valuable sublimation, or an ineradicable craving; but it is obvious it cannot be all three at once. Where religion is regarded as an undesirable complex, which must be brought to consciousness and dispersed before mental peace can be found, then naturally it is traced to something deeper, and generally to a disguised craving of another order, and therefore to one of the fundamental instincts. Because it has been believed by one school of psycho-analysts that sex is the fundamental instinct, religion is by them thought to be entirely traceable to that instinct. The evidence which has led to this explanation is, amongst other things, that puberty and religious conversion take place about the same time, that religious inhibitions and the sex instinct are in constant conflict, and that the higher forms of religious experience found in mysticism frequently use expressions borrowed from the sexual realm. But in reality none of this evidence proves, or even suggests, that religion is only the sex instinct in another form. The fact that the two things should often come into consciousness together is only natural, since it is at that time that the individual

THE INSTINCT FOR RELIGION

becomes strongly conscious of himself and of his needs; intellectual or artistic interests are often awakened at the same time. The fact that religion and sex are so often in conflict hardly indicates that they are really the same thing; on the contrary. Very few psychologists would advocate that sex craving must be given indiscriminate and immediate satisfaction, for this would make social life impossible; and nearly everyone has some sort of interior inhibition against this, which, although it is often referred to religious ideas, is probably due to something as instinctive as sex itself; for among the animals, when in a natural state, sex is strictly regulated, and since it is believed that we have inherited our instincts from the animals, we should expect inhibitions also to be inherited. It is found, however, that if the sex instinct is to be properly regulated, it must be not by repression, but by sublimation; and for that religion is most effective. Since religion has this power, it is surely much more natural to conclude that religion is the only thing which can ultimately satisfy even the sex craving. For it is to be noted that where in ideal marriage the sex craving is best satisfied and regularized, the religious craving can still exist; indeed, it is often where there is irregular and excessive indulgence that the conflict with religion is so strongly felt. The fact that sex language is sometimes used to describe the highest religious experience, and yet that some of the highest forms of this experience have been reached in celibacy, surely shows that religion is the final satisfaction of this craving; for, on the hypothesis that the sex craving is so insatiable, which psychologists are driven to admit, it is difficult to believe that religion is only a disguise of that craving; for this is not a craving which is likely to be satisfied with mere pretence. Moreover, the obvious

THE INSTINCT FOR RELIGION

purpose of the sex craving is the continuance of the race, and for that religion alone can offer any worthy end. We might as well refer the craving for God to the craving for food; for we find exactly the same language derived from hunger and thirst and its satisfaction used of religious longing and experience. The sheer nonsense of such an argument would be, however, too apparent. For men do not long for God only when they are hungry; hunger often shuts out all such ideas; and certainly the satisfaction of hunger does not satisfy the desire for God, it often awakens it the more; although the over-satisfaction of hunger in making eating the very end of life operates in just the same way as irregular sex indulgence in clouding religious consciousness.

Long before the rise of modern psychology religion had been traced to fear. But this is at best only a superficial explanation; for we have still to enquire where fear comes from; and religion is the only thing that will take final fear away. This old explanation of the origin of religion at least contradicts the popular idea that it is religion which creates man's fears; and it is being discovered that when definite religious beliefs have been abandoned under the pressure of modern scepticism, the old fears still remain. The fear of annihilation can apparently produce a worse panic than the fear of hell; and the fear of hell can be found even where there is no belief in God, but where belief in immortality still remains. Even when immortality is doubted or rejected, men can fear that they are going to get the experience of hell in this world, and sometimes their actual mental condition hardly falls short of the most extravagant imaginations of what hell is like. The absence of religious faith which characterizes our age holds out no promise of destroying man's fears; indeed, the more man becomes conscious and cultured and faces

THE INSTINCT FOR RELIGION

the situation with which atheism leaves him confronted, namely, that his consciousness has emerged in a world which can never satisfy it, the more his fears will increase and become the dominant fact of conscious life. Only in the belief that there is an Eternal Being who is the anchorage of all our aspirations, not only for continued personal existence, but for moral progress and satisfaction, can man get rid of his fears.

This explanation is confirmed when we consider the relation between the acquisitive instinct and the desire for God. Man always wants to gather to himself something other than himself, and at first he thinks he will be satisfied with the possession of things. But when he has all these around him in abundance, and has reached, as far as is humanly possible, a complete insurance of security in his possessions, he still finds himself unsatisfied. Man does want something other than himself, but that something must not be merely other but also more; it must be the possession of a principle of life beyond destruction or loss, and that can be found only in immortality, and in that type of immortality which the Christian religion calls eternal life, that is a life in union with God. Therefore the modern therapeutic psychologist is almost bound to recognize religion as the only compensation for desires in man which cannot be allowed their unlimited satisfaction; not only because other people have the same desires, and all cannot be satisfied alike, but because there is no unlimited satisfaction save in God. The social inhibition of the rank individualism of human instincts must either repress them, where they continue, as it were, to ferment, and at last break out in some form of nervous or mental instability, or they must be sublimated; and although art, or intellectual enquiry, or social concern are valuable means of

THE INSTINCT FOR RELIGION

sublimation, these depend for their highest exercise on religious inspiration, or when they are fully satisfied only leave religion a still more conscious craving. Therefore, the psychologist is bound to assume the objective validity of the religious idea; for if it ever came to be widely and completely accepted that religion was a craving satisfied merely with the idea of God, but that the idea of God had no objective reality answering to it, then the whole value of religion as a practical sublimation would disappear, and a conflict would gather within the mind of man of such depth, contradiction and intolerability as would utterly wreck his mind; and it is indeed with something like this that modern irreligion seems to be now threatening us.

There remains only one more explanation proffered by modern psychology which would dispose of the validity of religion; it is that man's conscious mind has a tendency to what is called " rationalization." This somewhat unfortunate term is used to describe the process by which we find excuses for actions, which we can then refer to rational causes, while they are really referable to unconscious, and therefore, non-rational processes. On this hypothesis all our theories are merely after-attempts to explain the existence of certain cravings within us. There is no doubt that this form of excuse is constantly at work in us, and that a great deal that passes for reason is nothing of the kind; but if this explanation were made universal, it must be noted that it would also dispose of this particular theory of rationalization, and of all psychological theories; for they in turn then become, as is indeed suspected in some of them, mere excuses for maintaining that the sex craving must be satisfied, or that religion is one vast delusion. This altogether suspicious and self-defeating explanation needs no

THE INSTINCT FOR RELIGION

further refutation than its own statement. The rationalization which we call religion is no mere excuse for the working of our instincts, for, as is admitted, it is often in conflict with them. God is the only explanation of the idea of God, however much higher God may be than our ideas. This is a rationalization in the more ordinary and legitimate meaning of the word; for it satisfies more than the reason; it satisfies not only its own craving, but all other cravings, too. It may be that the actual psychological process by which this is accomplished may be described as a projection of our personality, which gives rise to the belief that there is a personal reality answering to our highest, most embracing and persistent craving; but this would not discredit its value and reality, for this is how all our thinking is done; unless we are willing to discredit all thinking whatever, including modern psychological theory! We cannot contemplate the alternative of man remaining a creature whose craving for God must grow ever more insistent as he comes the better to understand himself and to face the situation of earthly life; for even if we were compelled to face that terrible situation, on the naturalistic hypothesis, which is the only one then left open to us, we should have to believe that this craving had been educated in man by processes which neither contain nor can satisfy it; a thoroughly unscientific conclusion.

We may conclude, therefore, that modern psychology has established the reality of religion as a craving in the human mind, and that this can only be satisfied by the belief that some reality answers to it. We are thus faced with the alternative either that there is an answer to this craving or that existence is a hopeless riddle, with man at its centre by some accident, whose only hope is to become more conscious of his hopelessness. This not only threatens

THE INSTINCT FOR RELIGION

insanity; it is insanity. On more rational and scientific lines, and now supported by psychology, we can therefore safely conclude that the instincts of man have been planted in him in order to make his whole nature tend in a certain direction, and that direction is the conscious enjoyment of God. If, therefore, we may not speak of the religious instinct we may speak of the instinct for religion, or, regarding it as something deeper than any instinct, the fundamental craving, brought to consciousness by the discovery that all the other instincts fail of their satisfaction unless this fundamental one is given the first and most important place. Religion is deeper therefore than man's consciousness, and may often be at work when man is quite unaware of it and has not yet awakened to his need. The more conscious he becomes, the more he will realize what his fundamental craving is, and when he makes the satisfaction of this the chief end of life, his instincts will fall into their right place and even contribute to the harmony of his nature and its resultant tendency towards God.

XII

COMPARATIVE RELIGION

RELIGION may be looked at and studied from many points of view, but in particular there are three main lines of approach that we may distinguish as the rational, the psychological and the historical. We may investigate our own thinking, and on the basis discovered and the postulates which have to be assumed, we may come to the conclusion that there is a God, and that man is somehow related to Him. We have found that rational thought establishes the existence of God, because He is implied in our reason, which we are bound to trust, if we are going to think at all. But however clear and convincing the belief in God arrived at by means of reasoned thought may be, we know, as a matter of fact, that this is not how most people come to believe in God. They find faith inevitable because of some inner experience, a profound feeling which may develop, slowly or suddenly, with or without great mental and emotional upheaval; and it is then the task of psychology to trace the origin of such interior feelings, and explain their suddenness, overwhelming character and the conviction that they come from a power outside the individual. We have seen that there is no reason to conclude that psychology can explain away religion by referring it entirely to interior movements of the individual mind, by which one or other of the great human instincts creates an emotional complex which is then illegitimately personified; but psychology is bound to assume that religious feeling is traceable to God, the ultimate Reality. But the religion of a great many people rests neither upon reason, for that is not their strong point; nor upon any great emotional experience, for they have never had such a thing; but upon the things they have been taught on the authority of others, and the influence of their religious environment; in short, their religion rests upon a historic institution.

Now, all teaching accepted on authority carries some reason for acceptance apart from the mere existence of such teaching, and all religious organizations go back to some origin and have had a history. It is an interesting and important inquiry to discover to what the ascription of authority can be traced, and how religious organizations have come to be what they are; and whether their origin and development brings confirmation or otherwise as to the validity and truth of religion. It must be immediately obvious that these three aspects of religion are inextricably intertwined, that the influence of all three is always at work, and that it is impossible to reduce any one aspect to a concealed form of the other. It is the profound religious experience of great personalities which creates a tradition and helps to induce a similar experience, but rational thought has been continually exercised upon the meaning of such experiences in their application to the more ordinary person, and so we get a system of theology. It may be that psychological experience and historical development only work out unconsciously in the person, or slowly in the society, but this development can be checked by conscious thought and shown to be implicitly rational. The theologian regards all three processes as essential to one another, and instead of regarding any one of them as reducible to any other, or each

COMPARATIVE RELIGION

process as capable of being explained away, regards each of them as containing within itself an essence which posits and constitutes a revelation of God, while their combined witness provides a basis of faith which is entirely trustworthy and valid. The trust in our rational faculties, which we are bound to make, compels the assumption that our minds have been given this capacity by that which is itself rational, namely by God. Man's interior experience, taken as a whole, shows us that his emotions, cravings and instincts can never be controlled, set in order or satisfied, save by the necessary idea of God, to which reason brings him, being accepted as real. The history of religion confirms that the observance of religion is vital for humanity, and that without it there would be no social order, no progress in art, philosophy or science, and no hope for the future of the world. It is this last point which we have now to establish by examining the history and development of religion.

The historical approach to religion is complicated by the fact that there is more than one religion in the world, that the different religions have had different histories, while the actual origins of some of them are lost in the irrecoverable past. Not only are there many religions, but they embrace such different beliefs, ceremonies and interior attitudes, that it is extraordinarily difficult to find a general definition of religion that will embrace them all. The different religions not only present a content of great confusion, they are often completely contradictory, and they are frequently in bitter hostility to one another; every consciously accepted religion declaring that it is the one true religion and all others false. What must be inferred from the widespread but differing phenomena of religion; what can be learned by studying their history; is there any underlying

COMPARATIVE RELIGION

relationship between them all; what light is thereby thrown upon their claim to be a relevation; and can we decide what is their relative value and their respective content of truth?

The preliminary to any answer being obtained to these all-important questions is to undertake an investigation on the lines of what is now called Comparative Religion. Comparative Religion is an almost new study; whether or not it can be called a science, and what exactly are the conclusions to be formed from it, are matters still awaiting decision. Comparative Religion, as its name indicates, is an inquiry into all forms of religion which exist or have existed, an attempt to classify them by a comparison of their ideas and forms, and the endeavour, if possible, to discover their affiliations and origins. The difficulty of making this subject completely scientific is that every investigator is bound to have a certain religious, or sometimes anti-religious, bias; and if a religious bias, it will generally be in favour of one of the great forms of religion. It is difficult, therefore, to secure a calm and impartial statement of fact, where the facts are the expression of the most fundamental emotions, cravings and beliefs of mankind; and often the person who claims to be entirely scientific and disinterested in his approach only betrays that he comes to the subject with a prejudice that religion cannot correspond to any reality. Moreover, as a strict science, Comparative Religion has nothing to do with appraising the value of one religion as against another; it is not its business to decide as to the objective truth of different beliefs, and even the question of the origin of religion is now often put aside as beyond scientific discovery, since it must go back farther than we have any means of tracing. Nevertheless, even when thus limited, Comparative Religion brings to light some

COMPARATIVE RELIGION

interesting facts. Its discoveries in the main bring out three important points. The first is the universality of religion, given a wide enough definition of what religion is; and a definition that seems wide enough to cover the various phenomena that ought to be embraced is that religion is a belief in the existence of higher than human powers, and the endeavour to come into relationship with them. Although it has often been assumed that a race or tribe has been discovered without a religion, further knowledge has soon dispelled this notion, and it is now certain that no tribe or people, however degraded, have ever been found or heard of that were without some form of religion. And the farther back we go into history, the greater and more dominating does the influence of religion seem to be. In earlier times, and among primitive communities, religion is universally accepted, and even now, when the rise of criticism of various kinds has so undermined belief, and social changes have so diminished popular observances, there is still no atheistic nation, and no community of any size can be gathered together without religion appearing.

The second discovery of Comparative Religion has been that, although religious doctrines are so different, the myths so multitudinous, curious and confused, and the rituals so diverse, strange and often apparently meaningless, there is a likeness so remarkable discovered between them all that it demands some common explanation. And it is an interesting fact that in religions which seem nothing but a mass of superstition there can generally be found on inquiry a belief in a supreme spirit, a god who is both creator and father, only he is felt to be too distant for human approach, and so he remains ineffective for religious purposes, and recourse is made to lesser gods, demons or ghosts. The third discovery is, that the more rational and highly advanced religions have gone through historical developments which often pass through the same stages and approximate to a similar form.

Now, what has to be inferred from these discoveries? Comparative Religion as a strict science may refuse to sanction any conclusions, but there are some theories which have been put forward which need to be considered. There have been many attempts to trace religion to something other than itself, namely to animism, to fetichism, or to magic; to ghosts or to ancestor-worship. It is obvious that not all these theories of origin can be true; each one of them has been put forward by distinguished students of the subject, only to be utterly demolished by someone else, and there is certainly no one of them which will explain all known religions. It is coming to be widely agreed that religion is not to be traced to a non-religious origin.

The interesting theory has been put forward that the earliest form of religion which can be discovered is always a ritual, but that why this ritual is observed the performers cannot explain, because they have never felt the need to do so. But after a time stories have to be invented to explain why ritual takes this particular form and why it is necessary. These stories are mostly in the form of myths, setting forth in naïve form the relationship of the gods, their methods of creation, or their adventures in visiting this world. Out of these myths it is believed that theology has grown up by a process which first of all takes the myths to be true, and then re-shapes them in the light of rational and ethical considerations. The evidence in support of this theory is that ritual is a very conservative thing and lasts long enough for different explanations to be given at different periods, and often goes on existing when all explanations have been abandoned. A careful examination of the myths shows, however, that they are all personifications of natural processes, and the ritual reveals itself to be an earlier mimetic representation of the same processes which the myths set forth as personal stories of the gods; the myths merely describe natural causality, the movements of the heavenly bodies, or the rise and decay of vegetation; and the ritual can generally be discerned to be an effort to imitate these processes in the belief that they are actually dependent upon it. This would trace religion to a belief in magic, but in view of the fact that both go on existing, and generally in open hostility to one another, most students of Comparative Religion believe that religious ritual and magic must both go back to something more primitive, though what this is they cannot tell us. But a more sympathetic and psychologically valid interpretation is surely necessary and possible. Although under most of the myths there can be discerned personifications of natural processes, some of the myths have been developed into stories which are not only artistically beautiful, as their Greek forms so well known to classical students, but they obviously set forth many of the cravings and desires of the human heart for personal gods and for redemption from earthly existence by communion with them. Again, ritual is simply a lower way of expressing the feelings of joy and of sadness, of oneness with nature, and the desire to find something beyond it more corresponding to human need. When men grow dissatisfied with crude and puerile myths, and try to construct out of them a rational and ethical theology, they are still obeying the same feeling that dictated the earlier forms of expression. So that if this theory is true, there is nothing in this developing effort to express profound feeling which necessitates that it is at any stage futile, or at its final stage false. For if the theological stage is false, and not final, as Positivism has suggested, but must be carried further to the metaphysical and abstract, and at last to the scientific and rational, why should this be regarded as final and ultimate truth, especially since it seems to have gone back to the beginning again in making man's highest thought nothing but a representation of impersonal natural forces? It seems better to explain the development as due to the fact that man has discovered that the imitation of natural processes does not satisfy his highest personal cravings, and so he constructs the myth, which is a story of persons, because man is beginning to feel that only that which is personal can be really higher than himself and can bring fulfilment and help. In theology, there is recognition that God must be one, to which man is driven by his own rational processes and by the unifying tendency of science; also that for God to be really higher than man He must be ethically higher, and man's relationship with Him must be governed by ethical considerations; so that if ritual remains, as in some form it always does, it must be governed by the same ideas; it must produce ethical effects or be rejected as false.

It is the suggestion of the dependence of the theological upon the mythical stage in the development of religion which gives rise to the feeling that theology is no more true than the myth. But this is first of all to forget that there may be something true expressed in the myth; moreover, behind the myth is the ritual, and the ritual expresses an irrepressible feeling of man for communion with something higher than himself. This feeling is too fundamental not to correspond to some reality, and reason tells us what the higher reality must be,

COMPARATIVE RELIGION

namely the spiritual, personal, ethical reality, to which is given the name of God.

A study of religious mythology reveals that there is a tendency towards monotheism; the myths trace the gods back to an original god, or they strive to arrange the gods in a hierarchical order, and out of this endeavour there often emerge three outstanding gods with a tendency to make them aspects of one; as for instance in the Hindu triad of Brahmā, Vishnu and Siva, behind whom stands the impersonal abstraction, Brahman. Further, many of the myths represent the coming of one of the gods to earth in a human form. Sometimes this idea of incarnation does not remain merely mythical, that is, a mere story which no one believes actually to have happened in history, but it attaches itself to a historic person. We have, for instance, in the Hindu religion, the semi-mythical but probably historical hero Krishna, regarded as an incarnation of Vishnu. In the Buddhist religion we have a still more extraordinary development. The founder of Buddhism, Gautama, probably never even called himself the Buddha, or the " Enlightened One "; he apparently did not believe in the continued identity of the soul, but only in a successive reincarnation of forces produced by each soul's good and evil activities, and he was practically agnostic about the gods, certainly believing that they could not be of any help to us in our task of freeing ourselves from the burden of existence, since they were under the same necessity. In the strict sense the system taught by the Buddha was not a religion at all, but an ethical and psychological process for escaping the burden of personal existence. Yet Buddhism has become a religion with its worship, prayers, ceremonies, its great temples with their crowds of idols and clouds of incense, and it has developed a theology in which

Gautama is proclaimed a Buddha, an incarnation of the supreme and eternal Buddha. But since Gautama himself, having attained *Nirvana*, is supposed to be beyond hearing his people's prayers, or visiting the earth again, other Buddhas are put forward who can hear prayer, and particularly another incarnation for the redemption of man is looked for in the coming of Maitreya. Thus, left to itself and by perfectly natural processes, we get a religion whose likeness in many respects to Christianity, and in its Tibetan form to Catholic Christianity, is remarkable, though, at least in the latter case, Christian influence is to be more than suspected.

But another curious development of the myths is to be noted in the direction not only of an incarnate, but of a suffering God. This can probably also be traced back to the derivation of the myths from natural processes, namely, to the fact that if the vegetation is going to live again next spring, it must first die. It is in the Greek mysteries that this idea comes into such prominence. These mysteries were probably very old Oriental rites, imported through Asia Minor into the heart of the Roman Empire just previously to the coming of Christianity. The old State Religion, with its somewhat distant and ethically unsatisfactory Olympian deities, was beginning to lose its hold, and men were looking for a new religion such as the mysteries provided. The secrets of the mysteries were so well kept that we know very little for certain about them; although some of them seem to have originated in mere orgies, as in the Dionysian mysteries, and others may have leaned to licentiousness, most of them seem to have been connected with the desire for immortality, and to have contained some idea that this could only be attained by communion with a god who made some ethical demands upon initiates. This communion was believed to be attained by the use of purificatory ceremonies; the watching of a simple drama which set forth the myth of the god being slain, descending into the other world and rising again; and by a participation in a sacramental meal. In the mysteries of Mithra the ethical demands are more obvious and paramount, and the likeness to elements in Christian theology, the similarities with the Christian Sacrament noticeable in some Mithraic sculptures, and the resemblance of incidents in the myth to events in the career of Christ, are certainly remarkable. But in the case of the Mithraic mysteries it must be remembered that their introduction overlaps with the arrival of Christianity; the two religions were for some centuries almost rivals, and if there has been affiliation it was without doubt an attempt on the part of Mithraism to approximate to the Christian religion.

It is obvious that conclusions are bound to be drawn from the comparison of this material, but there are a good many of them, and some are entirely contradictory and mutually exclusive. For instance, it has been hastily assumed that all religions are the same in essence, but this is expressed in different ideas and varying forms. To this it has been more legitimately replied that, on the contrary, while we find similar ideas and the same rites in different religions, the essence of the religion, the religious feeling and the ethical aims are often entirely different. It has been held by students of the subject who cannot be easily dismissed, that everything points to an original divine revelation from which all religions, save perhaps the Christian, have deteriorated; while equally erudite students have traced all religions to an original human superstition on which all alike depend. Therefore we are often faced with opposing conclusions: the one, that all religions are equally true, and the other, that all religions are equally false.

If this were the only result of the study of Comparative Religion, then we should be left in complete confusion and with irreconcilable contradictions; but this confusion clears up when this material is fairly compared with Christianity as a historical religion, and the facts of its origin and development are admitted. It will be admitted that Christianity, like the ethnic religions, has been through a process of development, but that development has been of a unique character. First of all, it does not depend upon unconscious processes, and the fashioning of myths, even if these have had their influence, but upon the movements inaugurated by historic persons, namely: the Prophets of Israel, the influence of Christ's personality, and the experiences of saints and the arguments of theologians, who regard Christ as their personal inspiration and the object of their worship. Secondly, Christianity, owes everything to a personal Founder, and like Buddhism, has also been grafted on to a previous religion: as Buddhism sprang from and assumed the Vedic religion of India, so Christianity springs from and assumes the religion of Israel. It is believed by many scholars that the religion of Israel goes back to paganism and to the primitive ideas common to heathen religions. This is of course not the biblical account, and the biblical account would seem to be preferable, if rightly interpreted; for there is in Israel's religion always an uncorrupted core; it is constantly at war with heathen infiltrations; it certainly does show remarkable correspondences with ceremonies and customs in other religions, but these are never

COMPARATIVE RELIGION

allowed to become perverted and superstitious. It retains their spiritual meaning, keeps this dominant, and, at length, in Christianity, finds itself set free from all that is merely legal, unworthy or superstitious. It certainly looks as if this religion has progressed while other religions have fallen away, or have lost their way and become stagnant, when they can only regain vitality by borrowing from Christianity, as Hinduism has certainly done. Christianity fulfils the prophetic promises when they are widely and spiritually interpreted, not only of its own Scriptures, but those contained in the mythologies of other religions; so that it is the true inheritor of all religions, carries out its line of progress to triumphant attainment, and is still capable of infinite development; neither being bound by nor contradicting its past, but developing its own principles, gathering to itself the contributions of growing thought, and applying itself with fertilizing power to every human problem and need. Therein it shows a unique and unparalleled movement the more it is compared with other religions.

The Christian religion fulfils what the other religions grope after, only promise or pervert. In drawing attention to the likenesses between the ancient myths and Christian theology, between the ceremonies of the mysteries and the sacraments of the Church, it must be admitted that the likeness is oftentimes very faint, and in popular works is often greatly exaggerated; but there *is* a likeness and some reason has to be found for it. Now, any extensive borrowing on the part of Christianity from heathen myths or pagan mysteries is inconceivable; here the intolerant exclusiveness of Judaism played a necessary part until its work was finished. Thus we are faced with a dilemma of astonishing importance: either we have to assume that the whole story of Christ is a myth, constructed as the other myths were, but this is absolutely impossible, for the historicity of Christ is beyond all reasonable doubt; or we have to believe that the myths themselves were a kind of prophecy of Christ. As man looked at the sky, as he watched the passing year, as he tried to express the cravings of his own heart, he found they always led him to dream of the story of an incarnate God, a Suffering Saviour who dies and rises again. Where the endeavour has been made to fasten a myth on to a historic person the incongruity is revealed. In the case of Krishna, he is himself too mythical and in character quite unworthy; in the case of the Buddha, his whole teaching is opposed to any such application. Now, it is remarkable that a non-theistic and agnostic religion like that of Buddhism should gradually have evolved a theology so like that of the Incarnation and the Trinity found in Christianity, but it has had to be done by a perversion of the Buddha's teaching and in express opposition to his fundamental ideas. But in Christianity the doctrine of the Incarnation and of the Trinity can be attached to the person of Christ because they are found already implied in the teaching of Jesus and give the only possible explanation of His consciousness, the demands He asks from men, and the power of His personality.

In that desire which has been found in all religions for some tangible representation of God, expressed variously in hero-worship, in the making of images, in the combination of a historic person with poetic mythology, we have a craving which is at last satisfied and entirely sanctioned by Christianity; for here we have a human form that it is legitimate to adore, because He is the incarnation of God. All that curious love for dramatic representation, the feeling for the sacramental significance of common things, which we find in all religions, although it often descends to idolatry and fetichism, is by Christianity neither surrendered to deterioration nor unreasonably forbidden, but is given its right place in a Sacrament that never fails to set forth the personal reality and the ethical demands of Him whose Sacrament it is. The endeavour to trace the Christian Eucharist to an adaptation by St. Paul and St. John from the heathen mysteries is a last hopeless attempt to resist the significance of their similarity, and is entirely unnecessary, since the seed and sanction of the sacramental idea is found not only in the actual Institution of the Eucharist by Jesus, but in His whole outlook upon life.

If this religion, which draws a straight line right down history to this hour, and promises still to continue by its own spiritual momentum, and which so wonderfully sanctions and satisfies the cravings which have given rise to all religions, is not true, then it is no use looking to other religions for truth; for they only dream and promise what Christianity makes living and actual. With the proving of Christianity false, they would be proved still more false, and then all religion must be ruled out of life as a phantasy and a delusion. Irresponsible persons have accepted this deduction, but apparently without considering what truth is then left in human history, whether the human mind is capable of truth, or whether truth has any meaning. With Christianity would fall all other religions; but there would be seen sooner or later the fall also of art, science, human service, and all hopes for the future of humanity. To hold that Christianity is true does not mean that all other religions are false: it means that the great truths they have lived by,

Christianity incarnates in an ever-living Person, which gives them greater power; the truths they have perverted, it rescues and restores to their right meaning; and the truths they have only been able to grope after, it at length sets forth clear and unmistakable. For the fact is that we should never discern the underlying meaning of the myths, the significance of savage ceremonies, or what was meant by the ideas which the higher religions have been striving to express, unless we had an embodiment of them to show the goal that they were seeking. When then we turn our attention to Christianity as the highest embodiment of religion, we are not narrowing our concern, we are giving all other religions a greater meaning than otherwise they could possibly have; we are taking the one line of truth through history that stands out clearly and guarantees that truth is possible to man because it is a divine revelation; and we are following a line which gathers to itself all man's cravings, redeeming and sanctifying even the things wherein he had gone astray. By following this line we find the only hope of reading any meaning into the history of the past, of focussing all earth's broken lights into one burning centre, and so of lighting up the future with illimitable hope.

For Product Safety Concerns and Information please contact our EU representative GPSR@taylorandfrancis.com
Taylor & Francis Verlag GmbH, Kaufingerstraße 24, 80331 München, Germany

www.ingramcontent.com/pod-product-compliance
Lightning Source LLC
Chambersburg PA
CBHW050636300426
44112CB00012B/1817